Your PhD

as a self-propelled

CATAPULT

Cosimo Buffone, PhD

Unthought Known Ltd

Unthought Known Ltd
6 Redheughs Rigg
Edinburgh, EH12 9DQ
United Kingdom
unthought-known@hotmail.com

Ordering Information:
Quantity sales. Special discounts are available on quantity purchases by corporations, associations, and others. For details, contact the publisher at the address above.

ISBN: 978-1-8382736-0-6

Printed in the United Kingdom

I dedicate this book to my sweet daughter Rosa Angela Emanuela for all the joy she regularly gives us and some of the unavoidable pain associated with her growing up.

Disclaimer

Both the author and publisher have made every effort to ensure that the information in this book was correct at press time. However, both the author and publisher do not assume and hereby disclaim any liability to any party for any loss, damage, or disruption caused by errors or omissions, whether such errors or omissions result from negligence, accident, or any other cause.

Additionally, the author has tried to recreate events, locales and conversations from his memories of them. In order to maintain their anonymity in some instances the author has changed or deliberately omitted the names of individuals and places. Furthermore, the author may have also changed some identifying characteristics and details such as physical properties, occupations and places of residence.

Contents

Preface / 1

Chapter 1. Qualifying session: Getting to the grid

Why should you spend your precious time reading this book? / 3

How does this book deliver immediate tangible value to you? / 8

Some general suggestions for every writing effort / 12

How did I end up in a PhD project? / 14

My journey as a writer and as a coach / 20

Which are my motives to help you succeed? / 23

Some statistics about PhDs / 25

Learning and coaching / 29

Project or Program Based Learning? / 32

The exclusive and unique relationship PhD student-supervisor / 38

My top tips for sailing through your PhD project / 46

Chapter 2. Warm up

A structured approach for sailing through a PhD project / 50

How to keep the initial mood lasting three years / 53

What is scientific research and how to conduct it / 57

Tips for sustaining body/mind during a three years long marathon / 74

How planning remains key to long term success / 78

Chapter 3. The race

The donkey's work / 100

The writing of your first book and quality thereof / 102

How to turn a rather dull thing into an advantage / 111

Attending conferences / 117

How to write an enlightening scientific paper / 121

Learning how to learn / 130

Concluding remarks on writing papers / 147

Publishing your first paper / 148

Chapter 4. After the Checkered Flag

From submitting your thesis until after your thesis defense / 154

Is the PhD an end or a new beginning? / 159

Further training / 164

Few more suggestions / 167

Want to become a writer? / 170

Bibliography / 175

Your **PhD**

as a self-propelled

CATAPULT

Preface

This book is a practical approach to managing a PhD project. It is written in the simplest possible terms and is a distillate of nearly twenty years of my professional journey. Having helped many students from different backgrounds understand what research is about and how to become passionate about the quest after truth, my new goal is to inspire you to do the same throughout this book's pages.

With this book, I like to think I am your coach, still mentoring you by example. There is no coaching without prior learning. And to learn, some limited mentoring is essential.

The writing style of this book is relatively informal. I do everything possible to portray myself as one of you, which means that I like to think of myself as a learner. A PhD graduate with some experience. A passionate researcher. But not at all your PhD supervisor. You have one or more supervisors already. You do not need more. Instead, I want to play a different role for you. And I hope I have literally squeezed the best out of me, for you to learn it as you move through the pages of this book.

We will analyze in some depth different facts and aspects related to the PhD project; however, my writing style is quite passionate and, at times, deliberately sharp. I use many metaphors, figurative language, and I use a combination of short, more extended complex, and compound sentences to intentionally produce an effect. Therefore, be prepared to be also inspired by language to reflect the experiences I went through.

The book is filled with real examples, where I used different combinations of tactics and strategies to achieve my set goals. Many sections of this book are infused with psychology. Through examples, I will show you how psychology plays a vital role in the rich human interaction of a PhD project. Psychology is particularly crucial for the PhD student/supervisor interaction, which is key to your PhD project's success.

Throughout this book, I assume that the PhD project duration is three years. Despite there are countries in which the standard PhD (or doctorate, as it is also known) duration is four years.

The structure of the chapters tries to follow that of the main stages of a PhD project. I compared it to a Formula 1 race to make it more visual and, at the same time, funny.

Finally, I really hope to strike a chord with both the book's content and the writing style. And my biggest hope is that you all find what I wrote informative, inspiring, and a bit innovative.

From the bottom of my heart, I wish you all GOOD LUCK in your pursuits.

Qualifying session: Getting to the grid 1

Why should you spend your precious time reading this book?

Not many students know exactly what a PhD is about. A good number of PhDs these days spend a considerable amount of time understanding why they are there, what they are doing, and why they are doing it?

This is a bit crazy, but it is the way it is. And it is widely accepted to be this way by almost everybody involved.

The only explanation I can give to this nebulous horizon a student is confronted with is that this of the PhD is a fascinating journey, and the student should define (more than find) a way through it. It is by carving a path past the initial confusion and overcoming the difficulties encountered all along the journey that a student character gets forged. And this is not a small thing at all. This is probably the real essence of the PhD project.

Needless to say that a PhD opens a door in a new world. With a PhD in your hands, you can travel farther and climb higher. These three letters (PhD) are a kind of door opening for many well-paid positions, both in industry and academia. For professional academia, a PhD is almost mandatory. Having a PhD also gives more status in society, and you will gain more respect as a recognized expert in your field.

More or less, you knew this already. So, which are the reasons you should be reading this book, then? And when should you read it? Without being arrogant here, this book is written by someone who had a somewhat successful PhD project. This book is also written by a PhD supervisor working as a Senior Researcher and then Associate Professor at some academic institutions around the World. The writer has also worked for around eight years in industry, mainly covering research and development roles and supervising several PhD students based at the company premises. Having seen both sides of research (academia and industry) and having experienced the immense pressures in rapidly changing industrial settings, the writer has felt an urge to give some structured and easy to follow suggestions to provide students with a framework. Yes, this book is no more than a scaffolding on which you can build your PhD project. Following this, the book also gives specific and concise examples of overcoming possible issues typically encountered during the long, at time tortuous, and fascinating path of PhD journey.

This book wants to be a sort of inspiration for all students who have made a conscious choice to invest three years of their adult life in such an undertaking. I probably speak the student mind here by saying that the choice is a very courageous one, as bold was my choice less than one month after 9/11 in moving almost at the blink of an eye from the Ancient city of Rome to lovely Edinburgh. At that time, that seemed a gamble to all of my original family members. It was not felt at all like this by me. The excitement was so big that it practically lasted nearly three full years. And you will experience some of that kind and long-lasting thrill as you turn with your fingers the pages of this book. You will be watching unfolding in front of your eyes one of the most enlightening journeys of my life to date. By understanding the choices I made and why I made them, I hope that you will be inspired by being equally, if not more, courageous.

This book is scattered with amusing anecdotes. They should provide you with inspirational examples to motivate you to achieve more, doing less, and using even less. This is the most crucial concept I am determined to elucidate on every single page of this book.

This book has been written with the idea that each part can be read separately. That means you can dive into each section without knowing what the previous and next parts cover. This approach comes very handily for those students who are towards the end of their project and might only need some guidance on writing the thesis or writing a scientific paper.

You can keep this book as a reference, guiding you through the different stages of the PhD. You can pull it out when you believe you are facing something stiff. Better though, if you give a good read at the start of your PhD, so you know that there is already some extra help at hand on your desk, should you need some at any stage of your PhD project. This book is like a wise man: patiently waiting for lending a hand, not arrogant but inspiring, not as a bible instead as a guide.

Your project is a long shot, a very long marathon, a potentially rather long and exhausting journey. You should reframe all of this, and I will help you 'see' how to completely change the perspective of this fascinating and enlightening long ride. Following this different approach from the very start of your PhD, you will soon realize how you can mold your project more or less the way you want. And if you achieve this, you will benefit from this first learning experience throughout your life, which is exactly what happened to me.

The book is more tailored to experimental PhD projects. However, many of the parts are also very much valid for numerical and analytical PhD projects.

If I had to condense in a single sentence the usefulness of this book, that sentence would probably read as: 'A friendly, concise, and discrete companion in a long, at time tortuous, but surely fascinating PhD journey that has the potential to change your life.' If I had to squeeze in a single word everything this book is, that would indeed read as: 'Empowering.' Similarly, if I had to squeeze in a single word, everything this book is NOT about, that word would definitely be: 'Waste.'

My mission is to share the relatively long experience, learning, and understanding I accumulated over the years with new generations of students to reduce as much as possible their waste of precious time, boost their productivity, and avoid unnecessary distress. This is especially true for two parts of the PhD project: 1. the unnecessary waste of precious time at the beginning of the PhD project, when some mist needs clearing as quickly and as permanently as possible; 2. and, the somewhat chaotic time towards the end of the project that most likely could have been spared from the student, if someone would have given the student a framework, such as the one found in this convenient book.

How does this book deliver immediate tangible value to you?

This book is written so that the critical steps of a PhD project are all taken care of. In addition to this, the book is filled throughout with positiveness and encouragement. At times some warnings are also dispensed to avoid that you make the same mistakes that I or others I know have made. Practical examples support all of these claims, and suggestions from my personal experience, the emotive description of which gives a human touch to the book.

Let's see how this book is structured. To help us visualize the different parts, we compare the PhD journey with a Formula 1 race. The standard Formula 1 race is made of a qualifying session in which the relative position of cars on the grid is defined. In this book's structure, we have Chapter 1 taking the student up until the second part of his/her first year. All of the sections in Chapter 1 are aimed at preparing the student for the real race. These are essential steps to take in turn, and the student gets the tools necessary to compete for the race that would come next. Chapter 2 is the warm-up that racing cars make about thirty minutes before the race starts. Here the student experiments with what s/he has learned in the qualifying sessions (Chapter 1) and gets ready to run. This might last until the early parts of the second year of the PhD project. The real race comes in Chapter 3, where the core of the work is done. Chapter 3's contents overlap a bit in terms of time with the previous part (described in Chapter 2) and lasts up to the end of the PhD project. Usually, the PhD does not end here. Even a race does not end with the checkered flag. There is the podium and then the press conference. After graduation, we are faced with existential questions about what to do now with a PhD degree. Now that we wrote so much, can we somehow continue writing? All of this is covered in Chapter 4.

Many of the examples given are basically taken from my long experience in research (both in academia and industry); genuine and down to Earth explanations are brought to light to guide you through the thought process (conscious or unconscious) I followed at the time. When I was faced with such issues back in 2001-04, I was right in the middle of them, watching a story unfolding in front of me. I had limited visibility of what would have happened because of my actions when confronted with essential difficulties to be solved or simply more benign issues that required me to decide the direction to take. However, I did not stand still, and I actively participated in writing the script of that story. And now I am unfolding that story in front of your eyes for you to use it as an imaginary lighthouse guiding you through both calm and rough waters.

This book shows you how emotionally involving a PhD can be and reassures you in many different ways of how fine it is for you to try out what you feel to be the right thing to do. On this point, I should mention that when you make a decision, there should NOT be any regrets afterward. No one could have predicted what would have happened because of the genuine choice you made. You should not beat yourself up at a later stage just because a decision you made a few months earlier turned out to have not been the right one. At the time you took that step, it seemed the right thing to do. And this is the frame of mind you should keep at later times. It was right back them even if it is not right now.

Of course, now you have seen what happened after you made that decision. But what happened and, to a certain extent, how it happened could not have been predicted. Most of what we do is not 100% down to the actions we take. We are part of our story. We are the masters of our story. But at the same time, our story interacts and is closely intertwined with the stories of so many other people around that we cannot accurately define its precise course. However, you can stir the course of your story, and this is what you should concentrate on. Try hard to stir your story and be less preoccupied with stirring someone's else story.

The book gives a practical approach to the topics covered. As already said, all topics covered have been inspired by real experiences the author had over nearly twenty years spent in research in both academic and industrial environments. The proposed approach on how to solve issues is highlighted, clearly explained, and fully justified. The complete thought process, which went down back at the time, is unveiled to comprehend better one of your peers' mindset taking those steps during his PhD project (2001-04).

Research is a long-term investment as planting a new tree, having a considerable time lag before fruits appear on its branches, and eventually ripe. You publish a paper now and will see the benefits of all the excellent work you did many years later. By the time you see the effect of your work, you have probably changed a few more jobs. This is typically not what happens in many other aspects of your life, including but not limited to most other jobs. But it is a reality that, for instance, psychologists face every single day. They work with a patient today, and they might never see the plants springing out of the seeds they planted in the patient's mind. They can actually see bad things coming out at first from the patients as these latter react, sometimes forcefully, to the changes psychologists try to implement with their proposed and, at times, tailored therapeutic approach. With time, we researchers will get used to this approach too. This process is incredibly emotional when you will have students or employees to supervise. You might never see the effect of your words and actions on other people. They might fight you at first for what you genuinely are trying to share with them. Months or even years might go by before they start seeing the benefit of the good things you have worked hard to pass onto them.

By far, the most important message that this book gives throughout is to show you how you should aim at 'learning how to learn.' Once understood, this approach goes well beyond the apparent 'narrower' scope of this book as being focused on PhD projects.

Some general suggestions for every writing effort

The most disruptive things that can happen to your imagination when you are writing are INTERRUPTIONS. Constant interruptions inhibit your ability to produce creative writing. On the surface, writing might simply seem as you are transferring on paper what you did in the lab, as a 'scribe' would do. But this is far, really far, way too far from reality when you are talking about a PhD. You are writing a story. You want to impress the reader. Above all, you want to feel proud of all the very hard work you did and the difficulties you overcame along an enlightening but strenuous and, at times, also tortuous path. This cannot and should not be done in a sterile manner.

Writing is an art like painting, sculpturing, composing music, etc. You want to feel fully immersed in the story you are telling. The more engaged you are, the more emotional connection the reader will feel. In some critical passages, you might even achieve the unthinkable: bringing your reader right in the middle of the scene you are describing. Therefore, when you are writing essential passages of your thesis where you feel deeply immersed, find a time when it is quiet to unleash your writing potentials. This might be early in the morning or right after lunch when people might take a short coffee/tea break or a break from talking by searching the internet at their desks. It is all the same for writing a paper as well.

I suggest trying your best to finish a section of your thesis or paper every day. Why? Because completing something you started, gives your brain a significant boost. When your day ends, you have a sense of fulfillment for having concluded a task, albeit you did not finish the whole thesis/paper yet. This is one of the common errors that most humans make when we work on a long-lasting project. We tend to be overly focused on the end goal and strive all along to achieve that. We forget that even those climbers who challenge Mt. Everest do not get up at the top of the World in one day!

It is imperative to give ourselves some form of 'gift' for having reached a goal. If I were you, I would simply feel great every time I would write a section of a chapter by going home and, say, take a shower than would ideally wash off the tiredness accumulated during that long day and then prepare a nice and succulent meal. Then aim to have something a bit more special when you finish each chapter. It is probably a meal with someone you feel connected with, maybe even buying for yourself a garment or giving anything else that represents a lovely gift to yourself for having finished something important. Like this, you will reward your brain for its endeavors, and it will produce powerful hormones that will boost your general happiness and sense of fulfillment.

This of your thesis might be your first book. It might even be the last book many of us will write, as our passions and interests might drive us away from writing books. Therefore, this might well be your solo chance to leave a written legacy for centuries to come. Make the most of this opportunity you have, as it is really precious and nearly unique.

Read some other PhD thesis and understand their structure. Find a thesis layout that suits your style more. And then comes the most laborious part: transform all those nearly mechanically produced data in the form of data points, maps, and schemes drawn on paper representing test facilities into the most important story of your life to date.

To fully accomplish this task, you would need to rely on a combination of determination, crafting, and some luck.

Welcome to the unique realm of the writers. We drive others by using words to build imaginary pictures in people heads and inspire them with one of the most powerful craftsmanship.

How did I end up in a PhD project?

As the story unfolds, you will grasp how sometimes luck gives a kiss to your forehead, and some other times, your inventive brain can turn almost anything into a huge advantage. Are you ready to learn the tale?

I went to the eternal city of Rome for an MEng in aerospace engineering because my girlfriend was thrilled about this field of science. At first I was not that fussed about it, but from the third year on, it really took off the ground, and I loved every single module I took since then. When I graduated, I went for some time to the air force for what was back then a compulsory ten months service. After that, I accepted to remain with one of the supervisors of my master thesis for six months teaching a numerical code to his students and editing his first book in fluid dynamics. Following that, I signed a one-year contract with the Italian Space Agency through another of my supervisors. I did not finish this second job, though. Over the spring of 2001 (before I started the second job at the space agency), there was an inevitable turmoil between my girlfriend and me. I wanted to get a permanent position in industry (most likely away from Rome), and she wanted to remain in Rome.

One day she literally proclaimed: 'You should get a job in the UK. I will follow you there where I can also get a master.'

This prospect was tempting, but my level of English was not that great. I signed for another English course and started applying to PhD posts in the UK. My first attempts to get to England failed as I could only get the fees paid; as European, I would have had no salary whatsoever. A young professor from Warwick I applied to suggested me to look for PhD posts in Scotland where, as European, I would have also received a salary.

Of the applications I made, one was at The University of Edinburgh. I must have applied there in June 2001. During the same month, I had started working at the space agency. We had only one Motorola 'brick' type mobile phone in the household, the one with a flipping mouthpiece and an extractable antenna. It usually rested on the fridge, and we took it out of home only when leaving the house together for long spells; so small it was!

One day toward the middle of July, I recall well that I had to return home over lunch to get some phone calls sorted. And because of this, I asked my boss's permission to have lunch at home as well. I took tram number 19 in Rome, and in around twenty minutes, I arrived home in the San Lorenzo quarter close to Termini train station.

After making the calls I was there to do, we started preparing lunch. I still remember to have been around the sink, washing some vegetables, and the phone rang. I wiped my hands and picked up the black brick Motorola phone with a red cover. Someone talking in English was speaking from the other end of the wire. My girlfriend must have frozen by then at the English words coming out of the handset; she was speechless. His English was perfect; he sounded very calm; and, the words he spoke were unambiguous. Because of my not so good English, it took me a little while to figure out what this gentleman referred to, but then he stressed that he was calling because I applied for a PhD post.

My insecure speech suddenly became broken, and my legs started having issues sustaining my weight. My earlier broken sentences become single syllables like 'yes' and 'ok.' The good thing is that not long afterward, this kind man told me he would have fired some information about the PhD project via email. What a relief at last! Even before he hanged, those shaking legs became two solid and straight boosters of a rocket engine. In less than he could say 'bye for now', I felt so light that upon watching below to see how my boosters were doing, I realized I was in orbit already!

My girlfriend had not said a single word and was sat now on the yellow bench by the side of my working station, which I had to carve in an angle of the tiny and crowded kitchen by assembling the wood I bought myself. We lived in a cozy apartment of circa thirty square meters on the first floor of via Tiburtina 180, one of those old buildings where Italian filmmakers had shot some pretty famous movies around WW2. In the quarter where we lived, there was still a small film studio in the basement of the next building down the road.

Before she asked who that was, my voice came back to normal, I orderly landed on Earth, and I told her about the gentleman and why his words made me so light, sent me so far, and for so long. Now it was her to lift from the ground, and before she disappeared, I grabbed her for a never-ending hug. It felt as we were glued! On that particular day in which I had to return home over lunch, in that tiny but full of outstanding and not so great memories, and no long before our summer holidays, we had now something to think about. For the rest of that day, I felt like walking on air. I went back to work, and a few hours later, I searched the internet, and I had received paperwork to fill and send back to Edinburgh. There was only a small but for me, potentially tricky hurdle. I had to take an English exam to show I could handle the language for doing a PhD. I booked the exam with the help of a colleague at the space agency who had a credit card (at home, we did not have a credit card at all at that time). Less than two weeks after, on August 2nd, I sat the test. The results were not that impressive but good enough to be accepted by the university.

Before breaking for the summer holidays on August 8th, my future supervisor wrote to me and asked if I could improve my English language skills. I talked to my girlfriend and agreed to go for the second year in a row in charming Dublin at an English summer school for two weeks. During our stay in Dublin between the end of August and the beginning of September, my future supervisor also called me. That was nice of him making sure I took the right steps to start my PhD on the front foot.

We came back to Italy, I told my current boss at the space agency that I had accepted an offer for a PhD, and I would have left at the end of the month. After my announcement, we witnessed alongside the whole World the vicious attack on the World Trade Center. With the shock of that event, which we saw unfolding in the office, I prayed for the people affected and hoped that everything would have been fine for our move. It was a bit sad to leave this work as they were preparing the space mission Corot, and I was heavily involved in this. Plus, one day, they had a high-level meeting about another project on a mission to Mars. I sat along with another young lady at the corner of a table where Italian Noble Prize winner Carlo Rubbia was present and giving an update of the project he led, funded by the Italian Space Agency. My master thesis project was on this idea of Prof. Carlo Rubbia, so I knew the background of that meeting. I saw firsthand how bright but, at times, strong characters, this sort of great minds are. My takeaway from that meeting was a red-colored lighter Prof. Rubbia left on the table, which I kept with me for the whole nine-year duration of my stay in the UK. I lost this lighter in 2010 during the process of moving our belongings out of the UK.

The excitement grew as we approached October 3rd, 2001, when we bought flight tickets with carrier KLM from Rome to Edinburgh with a stopover in Amsterdam. We had to move an entire flat full of things from Rome to Southern Italy, where our families live. That was an undertaking. With some help, we used my father's pickup truck and moved everything out. I went back and forth two times in two days, but I drove alone only on one return trip. One of our cousins kindly drove the pickup for the first return trip.

What I remember of Edinburgh is that we landed on Saturday afternoon. We stayed at a guest house in Costorphine and took a bus to the city center and then another to Leith, where I had booked over the internet (in writing and by email back then, which I could only use at the computer lab of the university in Rome) the viewing of a flat. There was something strange in the air as we approached Edinburgh city center. When we were around Murrayfield Stadium, an intense scent permeated the bus. I thought it was from bakeries. We saw the flat, we liked it, and we agreed to take it. We signed the contract, and on Monday morning, we moved in by taxi. On Monday afternoon, we paid a visit to King's Buildings campus and met my supervisor in person for the first time. He kindly prepared a cup of tea for my girlfriend and me in what would have been the coffee room of Kenneth Denbigh Chemical Engineering building, where I would meet with other inhabitants at 4 pm each weekday. I was quite pleased to have made it all way up there in Scotland and down to King's Buildings campus. However, there was still that pleasant scent that reached my lungs, yet I did not know what it was.

Only later in the week I was able to ask, using my limited English vocabulary, a lecturer of Greek origins what that scent might have been. With a grin on his face, he said that my guess was as far as from reality as Pluto is from the Sun! He revealed that what I inhaled was a mix of the Angel Share of the world-famous yellowish juice made in Scotland and beers from local breweries.

It would have taken nearly five months more for me to pour through my throat that flameless yellow fire. And before going to Scotland, I did not drink any alcohol whatsoever, plus I was like a gentle and innocent toddler drinking only water and milk.

I felt thrown by a cue stick from the Southern to the Northern end of a greenfield called Europe. And on reflection,

I happily admit that I like them both despite the vast differences between these two opposite ends. They both contributed enormously to the development of a human being. The invaluable know-how that this human adsorbed from these places went to forge his 'educational genes'. Those genes that come only after the real inherited biological genes from conception and the learned psychological ones from childhood.

With this short opening, I let you imagine the rest of the enlightening experience and yet eyebrow-raising cultural shock I went through in lovely Scotland!

My journey as a writer and as a coach

In this session, I will show you how I ended up pouring serious effort into becoming a writer and a coach. Hang around, and you will be amazed to learn what I learned of myself over the last few years.

I have always been a kid with a tremendous sense of purpose. Throughout my life, I continuously measured myself against tough challenges. Many of such difficult obstacles were set by myself. Many more had been set for me. And these latter have been the ones which have truly transformed the way I lived.

It is a known fact that our life mainly follows a steady slope upwards with the occasional falls; some of these falls could be prevented, and some others only predicted. I had no single fall that was either preventable or predictable. This means that I was aware of all my falls despite what I felt and said at the time. It was during these falls from grace that the most crucial leap forward came. During some of such times, I learned so much that my experience and learning resulted in deep understanding. And as I grew up, experience plus knowledge turned into wisdom. It is when I started mastering wisdom that a subsequent step became almost a necessity. This step is called a legacy. And here I am. My new appetite for writing comes just from an urge to leave a legacy. A legacy is not something I would be proud of, preferably something many people might benefit from.

If I am writing the other book after my PhD thesis, I feel an urge to share what I have understood (experienced and learned). In reality, it is the third book, because I also wrote a substantial Master thesis, but that one never got published (despite a conference paper exists that summarizes part of it). My PhD thesis is available in my former university and even on the ProQuest database. I am also writing in different genres: starting from short fiction stories for kids and psychological thrillers. Words appear almost daily on the screen in front of my eyes. I feel that a continuous flow of ordered thoughts and ideas makes its way from my mind to the screen. And this is hugely rewarding.

But I will not only write. I want to do much more than merely writing. Writing in itself is very important for both the writer and the readers. However, for a 'can do' person like me who likes to get his hands dirty, I cannot stop merely writing. I see this book as a flagship for a much broader set of tools that I am developing to assist the PhD student community. This is a large and complex plan which will surely take some good time and effort to see the light. However, I am very determined and will do all it takes to get to the place I want it to be.

How much is a book worth? I do not think anyone can put a price on any book. Where should we start from? From adding the costs to produce the book? And what about the benefits that it brings to readers. These will never be quantifiable. A writer writes to be heard. A reader reads at the very least to hear and at the very best to listen. When the reader listens, then s/he will try hard to implement what s/he has learned. Writing is eventually transformed into sound, that like music has a better chance to be passed on without deviations when written. A good book is much more valuable than the paper and ink used to print it. Some books impact people's life so much that these latter experience dramatic changes. Fewer books are so transformational that they can affect an entire nation or even part of the World. There is no fair price tag that can be put on a good book, let alone the other kind of transformational books described above.

And this is one of the reasons I like to write. My papers first and now the books I am writing are the distillate of my work and reflect my spirit's essence. I hope to reach as many of you, PhD students, as possible and that you will find what I wrote in this book inspirational for your project and, even possibly, a bit transformational for your future as a whole.

22

Which are my motives to help you succeed?

Let's talk straight about this! During the entire duration of my experimental PhD project, I always felt I was almost having a 'walk in the park.' It was not easy, but the right frame of mind and a supportive supervisor made climbing that colossal mountain, lasting less than three years, looking like more of a nice walk on an attractive green hill with a gorgeous landscape.

The only day I remained in the office until very early the next morning was the day I started at 8 pm printing the multiple copies of my thesis, which eventually I finished around 2 am. By 2.30 am, I had reached home on foot. Apart from that night, I never arrived in the office before 8:30 am and surely never left the office after 6 pm.

I performed a substantial amount of experiments in the process, having learned to use three very different and complex experimental techniques. I even did some limited work in my third year on numerical studies. I had practically finished my lab work by the end of the second year. My supervisor was not feeling good at seeking permission from the university to let me graduate before the two and half year mark. Therefore, I agreed to perform some numerical work as extra to keep myself occupied. I submitted my thesis just after two years and seven months from the start of my PhD and eventually sat my thesis defense two months before the end of my third year. I wrote my thesis in two and a half months and, apart from the length, it felt much more comfortable than to write one of the eight papers I wrote in connection with my PhD.

Do you think I am a 'special' kid? Do I have supernatural powers? Can I go for days without sleep? None of all of this! I played football, jogged (even in rainy Edinburgh sometimes), and regularly hang around with my fellow students and some of our teachers. I had a long-term girlfriend at the time, and we had a life full of activities.

If I did all of this, it is because, first and foremost, I like to think I have so much passion that I can sell it, without sounding arrogant here. I was also extremely determined to make it through the PhD as I wanted to have an industrial career. And, I was fully prepared to take myself through the twists and turns that any long term project is usually full of.

And now comes the WHY. Why after more than sixteen years since I got my PhD, I want to dedicate a good chunk of my precious time to helping others. The simple answer is that people with higher education tend to 'pull' many other people once they get into the marketplace with their specialist knowledge. Suppose these same PhD graduates have also mastered skills such as self-discipline, know-how to portray ideas and condense results in influential papers, thesis, time and project management skills, and are aware of some people management skills well. Thus, PhD graduates have the right mix of expertise and knowledge to be of paramount importance in our society.

I have done all of that. My PhD has been the single most truly transformational time devoted to acquiring critically essential skills. But also in forging a completely different mindset, which has allowed me to broaden my horizon. Over time I even learned sailing through very rough patches of the sea with almost no visibility in front of my eyes.

I want to inspire you while tending a helping hand in solving specific issues you might have on your project. This practical book's long-term goal is to empower you by making sure you master how to make your this project a success no matter what the difficulties you might encounter. To make sure this persists throughout your life, in this book, I will show you how I went about 'learning how to learn.'

Some statistics about PhDs

The Times Higher Education published some data in 2013, showing the completion time of PhD in England for students from the UK and EU (https://www.timeshighereducation.com/news/phd-completion-rates-2013/2006040.article). This report showed that nearly over 1/4 of the people enrolled do not finish their PhD within seven years. And with those who will complete their PhD by 25 years, the percentage increases to 80%.

This is a dire situation that impacts all people and institutions concerned. From the look of it, it is not much better than what it was back in 2004 when I finished my PhD. By far, the most significant negative impact is on the student. S/he has invested an enormous amount of time, energy, not to mention the lost income. Indeed, there are cases in which the student has enrolled in a PhD project because s/he did not find 'better things to do.' However, most of the PhD students enroll because they have genuine intentions to get a PhD qualification.

The fact someone is determined to get something is already a great start. A PhD is not a small thing, though. It is a particular type of degree in which you need to show motivation, independence, creativity, endurance, and perseverance, among many other things. Above all, there is a shift of attitude passing from a Master degree to a PhD degree. During the master course, you will learn subjects you need to repeat when you sit down for an exam/test. This is not the case for a PhD program. Here you might have some initial courses to follow and tests to sit; however, for most PhD programs, you will not find a book, a paper, or a website in which there is a written solution to the problem you are trying to solve. You will need to understand the problem well and use both your existing know-how and inventiveness to develop creative answers to your questions. Not everyone has this mindset. Admittedly, most people can change their

perspective. However, this switch might be more or less demanding, depending on the personality traits of the students. Openness to experience, agreeableness, and even some extraversion are three of the Big Five Personality Traits (https://en.wikipedia.org/wiki/Big_Five_personality_traits)
which usually help in a PhD project. If you have them in the right quantity, it might help you a great deal to succeed in your PhD. Being open to experience in practice means that you have the right attitude of a curious mind and might even have the right mindset for being inventive; this trait will help you accept changes in work settings and interpersonal relationships. Being high in agreeableness means that you are rather friendly with others and compassionate when required. This trait makes you likable to others, and therefore it is more likely that others will like and help you as well. Too much of it is not a good thing, though. Being too much agreeable means that a person can be easily manipulated, and this goes against the independence that every PhD student should demonstrate. A bit of extraversion also helps as it signals that you want to reach others and display high energy (physical and mental), which usually attracts others. Here I do not want to say that those scoring low in openness, agreeableness, and extraversion would not get their PhD. Not at all. But these latter might find it a bit more challenging because the PhD's nature requires some degree of such three personality traits.

I have always been aware of the relatively high dropout from PhD programs and the late finishing. Therefore, one of the motives that have driven me to put together this book is the feeling that most PhD students need just a bit of guidance and inspiration through those difficult times they encounter along their path. A smaller percentage of these students, instead, need a bit more structure and more sustained support.

This book is conceived to be a sort of reference each student can use throughout the PhD program. And typically, this is more than enough to reach, with some reasonable effort, the end of the PhD. This is because you already have at least one supervisor who acts as a mentor for the program's entire duration. In case you deems that more guidance is needed, then you should consider also exploring other options such as coaching outside of the university.

A PhD is almost a mandatory qualification nowadays to enter academia. PhD graduates are also highly welcomed in the industrial sector as directors of companies. Therefore, the program you are enrolled in gives you unparalleled access to many specialized jobs that are off-limits for many people out there.

As a PhD graduate, you are expected to learn the way you can conceive an idea, build on it, produce a plan (technical and financial), and apply for funding. If you win the bid, you should be able to recruit staff and deliver on the promises you made in your submitted proposal.

This can seem straightforward to some and arduous to others. What I can say is that there are several skills you will acquire throughout your PhD program. You will learn what the scientific method is and how to successfully apply it to get the best possible results, with the least possible effort, in the shortest possible time. You will also learn how to communicate at all levels. In fact, you might be assigned some master students to supervise and help. Then, you will communicate daily with other PhD students. And finally, you will interact with your supervisor and also other members of staff. You will learn how to interact with suppliers with activities such as producing a specification of what you are looking to buy and getting some competitive quotations. After this, you will liaise with the finance department to raise an order once your supervisor has approved your quote selection. The ordered equipment will arrive at some point at your university, you will check that the contents are not damaged, and the items you bought are working fine. You might be requested to bring the items to university technicians and put on them a tag as university's property. At this point, the buying cycle closes, and you have learned an import process that happens all the time in industry as well. You will learn technical skills that are specific to your project. Some of these have low transportability, whereas many others are transportable to other fields/jobs. They will become part of your portfolio, and some can even be transferable skills. This means that you have significantly increased your employability because now you can train others on that particular transferable skill. There could be some small grant applications within your university or external bodies, and I strongly suggest applying for them. It is not only that you might get some small amount of cash to buy something for the lab (hardware or software). But also because typically, these small grants are stripped-down versions of larger grants that you might be applying to once you finish your PhD and seek a career in academia.

I did not recruit anybody during my PhD project. However, I was asked along with few other PhD students to sit the interview day of aspirant lecturers, and in one case, we also had the chance to put questions forward to the interviewees. We were given a piece of paper and a pen to put down our impressions, and later, during the evaluation process, our opinions were also taken into account.

These are all essential stages that might seem minor from a distance. However, they are there for you to grab and experience them in full. Without overdoing it, you should actively participate in the life of the department that hosts you. You will see that over time everybody will start liking you. This also helps you feel 'part of' that reality, and the sense of being part of something is quite reassuring.

Cosimo Buffone

'Without learning, there is no coaching.'
From Becoming a Professional Life Coach
P. Williams and D. S. Menendez

Learning and coaching

That sentence from Williams and Menendez's book condensates in a few words the essence of coaching for PhD students. It is valid for all types of coaching. The coach should not interfere with the coachee's ability to develop the path to achieving sustained success. The role of the coach is to keep a fast-moving train on track. But for what concerns where the train wants to go and if the train wants to make some stops along the way, it is all down to the driver (i.e., coachee).

It is probably helpful to think of a coach as a lighthouse. It guides the sailor but does not sail for him, even in stormy waters. An excellent coach will work steadily to deliver a 'transformational learning experience' for the PhD. What does this mean? In simple terms, it means that the PhD will learn how to leap forward on his own over time.

The PhD student will experience a kind of vertical transformational change typical of the different development stages of humans. Coaching is not an incremental change. It is a radical new way of doing things. For some coachee, this change might well be considered as a real paradigm shift.

You will have grasped by now that to achieve such a target, the coachee (PhD student) should spend some good time and good energy in the learning process. This means learning about techniques as much as learning about oneself. When a coachee comes out from the other side, the transformation is rather profound, and, in most of cases, it is also lifelong. It goes without saying that few individuals find the coaching experience so transformational and empowering that they might well consider becoming a coach themselves at some point in their future. This is exactly what happened to me. Coaching is not only a mere job. Coaching is not only a passion. Coaching allows the coachee to see the World through the lens of more experienced eyes. And as such, over time, the PhD coachee will feel that the small door s/he was looking through at the Universe has become a boundless gate wider than the sight seen from his/her eyes.

At the very beginning, the coach will carefully assess the task at hand and the PhD student's resources. Later, together they will draft a preliminary plan to be discussed and agreed upon. Following that, which is already an achievement on its own, the coach might suggest some specific and timebound learning activities the coachee should do. They will then move swiftly to tackle the task, now feeling full of energies and guided by hope, and the coachee will hit straight the target as an eager arrow pointed through the sharp eyes of an eagle and effortlessly shot through a very loaded bow.

It is important to note that the coach will NOT do work for the coachee. The coach cannot write any part of you thesis or proofread it, as a matter of fact. You should not think I will substitute your invaluable supervisor/s. But surely, I can add something valuable to the work of your supervisor/s. And given my long experience in people management (I have also been a manager in two UK companies for over six years in total), I might even be able to help you reframe your work relationships.

Why am I talking about coaching here if this is a book about the PhD project? Well, coaching can also be delivering through how a book is written. Suggesting principles to be inspired by and not following rules is the perfect approach for a coachee's self-development. This is even more true for a PhD student, the ultimate goal of whom is mastering at 'learning how to learn.' Therefore, this book underlining principle provides you with a framework from which to build the artifact you wish to. And because of this very aim, the book is your most adorable personal coach: non-judgmental, patient, and exceptionally far-sighted.

This book constitutes a vital reference for the coaching sessions you might want to explore if you feel the need. However, this book is written so that, especially if taken seriously at the beginning of the PhD, you should not need coaching sessions. Having made this clear, sometimes students might have specific requirements in some areas, and then coaching can be regarded as a powerful short term support to address those needs.

I like to think that life is 50% down to fate and 50% down to us. A PhD is much more skewed than that. Typically, it is 80% down to you and 20% down to all the rest. Before gaining it, a PhD is like a massive target sitting over there for you to miss.

I am incredibly determined to guide your hand on that bow and drop an arrow that hits the target you put your sight on, getting straight at its heart. This is what coaching is for me.

Project or Program Based Learning?

What kind of learning process are you enrolled in? PROBLEM BASED LEARNING or PROJECT BASED LEARNING?

You start WRITING on a blank piece of paper. It is like ploughing through a virgin field. It is as much scary as it is exciting.

I did not know what scheme I was playing back then (2001-04). I thought to have played relatively well, though. On reflection, now that I understand the game I played and how I played it, I must admit I also had some reasonable share of luck.

In later years and because of interaction with many students, I started realising there was a framework behind. And that has been possible because I started zooming out of that framework. I had reached higher ground, and my horizon was broadening significantly. Think for a moment as you are climbing an Egyptian pyramid. As you get up the massive shaped stones, you will see much more around you and feel to be more in control.

After so many years of climbing this almost infinite pyramid, I feel I am in a position to share with you my perspective. You will see through my eyes and listen through my ears. But, crucially, you will speak through your mouth, as you would need to adapt what I will share with what you are experiencing at those lower levels of the pyramid you are climbing, which is most likely a completely different pyramid than the one I am still climbing. And we communicate through the ink that, absorbing light, spoils the charmingly colorless of a virgin page, and we can probably agree that then all those colors bleed into one.

A PhD is the second important level of the learning experience, an almost paradigm shift in the lifelong continuous learning process that we humans are both faced with and are thrilled by. The first important level of the learning process arrives at the first degree. You have been repeating what the teacher told you and have multiple chances of being involved in many more innovative learning processes than I had been involved with during my time at university, which dates back to the start of the internet era. During my time, we had basically a single learning setting. That was the setting of the frontal lessons. Here an experienced teacher passes his/her knowledge to several students. It was not uncommon to have teachers who used that stage to push their agenda and, in some cases, even abuse others because of their status. There was little interaction between teachers and students, and we had to repeat what the teacher was sharing with us. The classroom size was also a factor: in the first two years of my university degree in Rome, I sat in a class split into two classrooms of around four hundred students each! With all the right intention, no teacher could reach students at a personal level with such a scale of audience. When I arrived just a few minutes before the class started, I had to sit very far behind, and I had difficulties seeing all the small writing of the teachers on the blackboard. Some students arrived at 6:30 am for the 8 am start to take the first spots next to the blackboard; they will occupy their own places and other spots for fellow students who will arrive later. There was a fight for the first spots because those students sat there had a greater chance of being noticed every day by the teacher.

Let's roll back a few years. In the first levels of the school system, students get alphabetised. Which means that they learn how to read, write, and make simple calculus. This goes back to the school model as conceived during the industrial revolution when there was a need to churn out people with such skills (reading, writing, and performing calculus). Things have changed entirely since and these three necessary steps are now confined to the first few years of the educational system.

Fast-forwarding of a few years, if we take secondary schools and universities, nowadays, the teacher-student relationship has almost flipped over. The teacher is there to guide and support the students in their self-development. The tools available (both hardware and software) are so many and elaborated that students have an almost infinitive choice. The searches that students perform can be done through their smartphones in any place and anytime they want. The search is done asynchronously; in fact, asynchronous are many of the resources available to their fingertips. This means that there is no such pressure to arrive so early in the classroom and take the first spots to see clear the teacher writing on the blackboard and be noticed by the teacher at the same time. The internet is full as an egg of data and information students can pick up from and be inspired by. The same caution of checking the source of the data and information that is valid for published/broadcasted content should be done for internet-based content. After reviewing the content source, the student should also check where the materials have been taken from, which means checking the references cited. This is also a significant factor, and students should be able to spot if, in the text they read, citations to trustable sources have been made.

One critical aspect of online content is that you are allowed to like or dislike it in most cases, leave comments, and it is not uncommon that you can even interact with the content creator, albeit to a limited extent. So, unlikely us twenty years ago, you have much more say on what you consume. I have witnessed cases in which, because of viewers' comments, a reporter has been changed by the online broadcaster. This was unheard of even a decade ago.

Let's hover between secondary schools and universities for a while longer. A sort of CRITICAL THINKING is now promoted at school by teachers and developed by students from secondary school onwards. This is an essential step in the creation of a 'researcher mindset.' Without critical thinking, the quality of a PhD output is hampered because most likely, the student will stop at a little progression of what has been done already by others. This was my biggest concern when I was about to finish my first degree. I felt not to have gained critical thinking to be able to come up with my own creations. Instead, a PhD student is supposed to make a 'significant contribution' to the field. Of course, such a critical thinking attitude can be developed at any time during a person's life. I did that during my PhD project. So, even if a student has not been stimulated well enough at school and university, then there is always a time when it can be developed.

At this point, it is useful to recap on two fundamental methods of the learning process. They are PROJECT BASED LEARNING and PROGRAM BASED LEARNING. We will give enough information about these two methods to understand where a PhD project fits in between these two realms. Let's define them first. PROJECT BASED LEARNING is a learning approach focused on the OUTCOME. PROGRAM BASED LEARNING is instead a learning approach focused on the PROCESS. Therefore, with Project Based Learning, the student (or group of students) is geared up to develop many possible solutions to a problem. This method is similar to a brainstorming exercise in which several options are generated and ranked in order to come up with the most cost-effective or plausible solutions. In the Program Based Learning, the student (or group of students) are much more concentrated on 'discovery' as they go along.

This different approach also means that the tutor/teacher involvement in the student learning process is very different. In Project Based Learning, first developed in 1918 by John Dewey and William Kilpatrick, (https://pdfs.semanticscholar.org/679f/6146dce2b5fb9927c2 1acdae176570157360.pdf) the tutor/teacher guides and monitors the different phases of students' work. Thus, the tutor/teacher delivers more frontal lessons and has more hands-on involvement. Students are engaged in solving real problems and strive to find answers through completing a project. In Program Based Learning, instead, the tutor is a kind of 'facilitator.' It is a student-centered approach to tackling a problem with no clear-cut answer. This sort of approach stemmed from medical schools. The students are encouraged to develop a viable solution to a specific problem; which empowers students much more than the Project Based Learning approach. Finally, Project Based Learning is typically multidisciplinary and lasts much longer; Program Based Learning, instead, is focused on a single subject and therefore is also much shorter (https://www.teachermagazine.com.au/articles/problem-based-learning-and-project-based-learning).

These two different approaches also have a dramatic effect on the learning experience of students. In Program Based Learning, students are more empowered because the tutor/teacher takes a step back and goes on the backstage; s/he would seldom intervene in those cases in which the student/s get stuck.

Now your question might well be: what does this have to do with a PhD project? On the surface, a PhD project follows the footsteps of a Project Based Learning approach. In fact, a PhD is typically multidisciplinary, has some set goals to achieve, and you are guided and supported by a PhD supervisor. The only difference here is that, in most cases, you are doing your PhD on your own and not as part of a team. That said, there are many cases in which the PhD project is part of a larger collaborative program involving from a few (2 to 3) to many (up to 10 or 15) partners. This is an excellent opportunity to work alongside other PhD students and, at times, also PostDocs. My experience, though, is that for the majority of the project, the PhD is still working on his/her own. This is especially the case because, at the very beginning, the student has to acquire a considerable amount of knowledge, and this requires reading/learning that is mainly done away from others. However, the PhD student is also supposed to become empowered and have a 'discovery approach' as s/he progresses. The supervisor in this frame of mind is seen as a kind of facilitator. This is typical of a Program Based Learning approach.

During the project, the PhD student will focus on both outcomes (Project Based Learning) and process (Program Based Learning). And this is the very reason why we are mentioning these two different approaches to learning here. As PhD student, I believe that you should pivot freely and smoothly between these two approaches, especially in the way you see the evolving relationship with your supervisor. At the beginning of the project, you might have to rely on your supervisor's input a bit more often. However, as you start putting your own wings, you pivot completely towards being a somewhat independent thinker.

Something associated to this topic of the learning approaches is that you MUST NOT wait for your supervisor to provide inputs, guidance, material, motivation, set deadlines, and targets for you to achieve. You should become your own master. And as such, you are fully responsible for what is happening in your project. It is your project, nobody else one! This is a simple, critical, and mighty thought you must measure yourself against. If anything goes wrong in your project, it is your responsibility to seek help and do whatever it takes to solve the issue. This is not your supervisor's project. It is yours. And yours alone.

The exclusive and unique relationship PhD student-supervisor

This relationship is by far the one that contributes most to a PhD project's success or failure. As this book is aimed at students, then the emphasis is placed on the student and how s/he can overcome possible issues with the supervisor.

Let's start with a fact! In most cases, the supervisor has chosen you among tens of applicants for the same post. Or in case you applied to the supervisor with a project you have proposed, it was still him/her that decided to take you on. This means, at least on paper, s/he thinks you have the pedigree to perform well on the job s/he wants you to do. If you have been 'honest enough' in your CV, then there is not the slimmest of doubt that you will be able to do the job.

Additionally, the supervisor has not only been a PhD student before, but s/he has probably seen many other students before you. Over the years, the supervisor should have acquired enough experience and knowledge on how to interact with students that s/he should feel very comfortable in his/her shoes. Finally, your supervisor is supported by a large organization (the university), a place where you, as a student, go for learning. It is not framed as a job, as such. Higher education is where the right attitude is that you should be educated personally and professionally to make that giant leap forward and become a leader in your chosen field.

If all is looking so great, then why many student-supervisor relationships stifle up at some point, and some even end up sour? Could it be the subject the student is working on? Could it be down to the demanding deadlines? Could it be due to issues with funding (which at times are indeed present)? While these matters play a role as stressors, my experience is that they are NOT the key factor. They might look like the initiators or precipitators but are not the critical factor. They might well be aggravators, but again not the defining factor.

There is a step we seem to have missed in all of this, and that is your deliberate choice to apply to some specific PhD projects and not others. This is probably down to matching your skills and expertise with the field in which the prospective supervisor works and the topic s/he is proposing. At times, it is not easy to judge if you are a good fit or not with a specific project's requirements. The supervisor is likely to have cast a wide enough net with the PhD project ad that s/he has deliberately not been specific enough. Understandably, the supervisor wants to get the best possible candidate for the project; this is specifically true from a technical standpoint. Your personal and social qualities might be a second-order worry for the supervisor at the selection stage. On the flip side, you want to get a supportive supervisor who is not necessarily the best in the technical field. A supporting and kind of hands-off supervisor will literally make you flourish. A controlling and overly critical supervisor would surely harm your development as a young independent researcher. You would want some guidance instead of being told all the time what to do and not do. You wish to receive constructive criticism and not coming off the meetings with your supervisor feeling sad, resentful, or even angry. At times, I was criticized, but my supervisor helped me navigate through the fog rather than towing me along. It was not only him, though; I was ready to accept his suggestions and, at times, his criticism. I knew his criticism was directed to my plans, actions, and even possibly my words, but, crucially, not at me as a person. We went along very well all way through because there was not even a single instance in which that personal space was violated. And this was achieved because of the continuous strive made by both of us to keep the professional and personal relationships a bit separate. Towards the end of my project, when I eventually started seeing the significant outcome of all our efforts, I realized that we practically had 'virtually rubbed' on each other to climb higher and reach further; without encroaching on one another. I had a significant motive to get an outstanding PhD done, and for this, I almost literally picked up his brain as often as I could. From his side, I was the first very successful PhD project producing a large amount of data and papers, something that helped a lot his career at that point as well. We both won by a large margin with my PhD, and this is how you should look at your PhD as well. If you win, your supervisor wins too. If you both win, your university wins as well; the university invests a considerable amount of cash and people time on your project. Not to mention the country and society as a whole; they spend much more than anybody else and have a vested interest in making you succeed. They invest colossal amounts of resources for everybody development; for you gaining the PhD, they have been investing in you for decades!

Then, what is the crucial factor of complicated relationships between student and supervisor? Having analyzed all the relationships I had with several students from different parts of the World while working in academia in the UK, Belgium, and China, I concluded that the most crucial issue is the one related to personalities. Personality traits are vital in establishing and maintaining a healthy relationship over time. Three years of close contact is a rather long time, indeed. If the personality traits clash, then there is a high likelihood of a strained relationship or even failure. This is also true between friends, family members, and romantic relationships.

You do not need to learn about psychology, but it is highly advisable that you seek help in your university when you notice that things are taking a wrong turn. Why is this? Among the general population, there are between 10-15% of people who have severe personality issues. These people are also found in academia. They are 'victims' of their past, and all others should have some sympathy for them and even empathize with their condition. That said, if their health condition is concerning, then they can become rather demanding and, at times, be very unreasonable with others. In a tiny percentage of cases, their situation has become so severe over the years that they are basically potentially dangerous to others. This situation is even more worrying when the balance of power is skewed. Between student and supervisor, the balance of power is really skewed, and a toxic supervisor could really damage a student if the relationship takes a wrong turn.

What to do then in such situations? The first thing to do is that you should not make the situation worse by engaging in power struggles. Instead, you should collect some hard evidence and then seek help within your university at the earliest occasion possible. Universities have special services tailored to students. They will not only listen to your concerns, but crucially they will mediate and take steps to allow you to continue working and, at the same time, feel safe and valued. All of what you will tell them is strictly confidential. So, there is nothing for you to worry about; you should have no fears of coming forward with your issues connected to your supervisor's relationship. Additionally, unless you commit a severe offense, no one can throw you out of the PhD project without a proper process being followed.

Stumbling on extremely difficult supervisors does not happen very commonly. In my whole career to date, I have seen it only once getting incredibly bad. It was so unfortunate that the health of the student was severely affected for years. He eventually recovered, but the scars were evident long after the working relationship had officially ended. The student can also have personality issues. But typically, this does not constitute a significant threat to the supervisor as the relationship is skewed in favor of this latter, to start with. Additionally, should the student badly misbehave, it is very likely that the supervisor would involve other people within the university from a very early stage. One way or the other, the problem would be solved more swiftly.

As I said, these are rare cases that can result in severe consequences for those involved. However, in most cases related to student-supervisor issues, the situation is much more manageable.

It starts with your understanding that your priority is to get a PhD. Your first priority is NOT to fix people, fix things, or fight the wind. If your main focus is always clear to you, then the other issues you face can be watered down more quickly. During your PhD you have a unique opportunity to make some changes to the way you approach things and people. For instance, when someone criticizes our work, we tend to take it as a personal level. This is normal, but we immediately react as someone was directly accusing us. This is NOT normal. During the PhD you will have plenty of opportunities to address this issue. A criticism on you must be direct. Otherwise, you might have just perceived it to be directed at you, but it was not. Let's take an example to clarify this point. Your supervisor can say one of the following as a comment on your poor performance at work:

A. You have done a terrible job on this experimental cell here.

B. This experimental cell looks awful. What happened? Can you tell me why?

C. This experimental cell could be improved significantly. Shall we discuss how?

See at the tone and the structure of statements A, B, and C. They practically say the same thing. However, the first statement is forthright (the word 'You' is the first in the sentence) and would hurt even my feeling, despite the strong character I like to think I have. Statement B is already rather good. The blame falls on the experimental cell, instead of you (the word 'you' appears very late, and it is not the focus of the criticism; 'you' is a vector by which your supervisor wants to learn more about why the experimental cell looks so terrible). Statement C is probably what every human being would like to receive as criticism. I have met people at different levels who can use a tone and a structure as the one on statement C in virtually any settings. This seems to be their natural attitude. While I strive to use statements like C, I consistently achieve statement B, and at times I also reach statement C. Your supervisor should be using at least statements like B. If you feel hurt about comments similar to statement B, then your sensitivity might be too high. In which case, you would need to work on yourself to improve this. When you finish your PhD, you will get other jobs, and there will always be criticism. It is not that often that people receive real and genuine constructive criticism. I also do not usually get constructive criticism. I learned, though, how to take that criticism (which sometimes is still really, really harsh) and turn it into an extra motivation. Few times this kind of harsh criticism leads me to some sort of 'breakthrough,' both in professional and private life settings.

Other factors will change as you progress on your PhD. These factors are not apparent at the beginning of your project, but you will undoubtedly feel as they evolve in later years. The first thing you would need to grasp is that when you start your project, your supervisor is the expert, and you kind of depend on him/her. As you get more familiar with your topic, you will notice the knowledge shifts more toward you. This becomes even more pronounced when you start building your experimental setup or start coding a numerical algorithm. At this point, the supervisor becomes dependent on you. In most cases, this dependent relationship is somewhat healthy, and the two of you reinforce each other. As you start getting results and analyze them to write scientific papers, you continue shifting toward becoming an expert. And you will undoubtedly notice that if your supervisor receives some visitors and they come to see your lab, then most likely, your supervisor will be happy to let you describe your work; because you are the expert now.

The last aspect I would like to underline is that when a student-supervisor relationship is healthy, then people close-by see it, and people further away hear about it. This means that when the sail has a tailwind, the sailor (you) will spring quite far ahead, and everybody will notice it. Therefore, you should have a vested interest in ensuring this special relationship with your supervisor is stable and resilient enough.

How do you make sure this is the case? Simple! You work on it. This is true of any kind of relationship. You need to spend time and energies to make it to work. Don't wait that the supervisor puts all the effort required. S/he could have many other students to supervise. This was certainly my case. He would come to see me regularly, especially at the beginning of the project. And then I also started paying some visits to his office, showing some impressive results or seeking some advice. I made some mistakes during my project, and he was always supportive, the same as my second supervisor. This has been one of the most important reasons I feel to have done a great job during my PhD project. And this seems to have had a strong correlation with the number of papers published during my PhD project.

It is quite typical that a busy supervisor would see you for, say, one hour per week. You might be the first PhD student of a young supervisor. In this case, s/he might have more time to dedicate to you. When I started my PhD, my supervisor had two other students. He was paying regular visits to all of us in the lab, sometimes every day. This seemed to be because he had a keen interest in what we were building in the lab. An experimentalist might be much more inclined to spend time in the lab, and therefore even as a lecturer/professor, s/he would hang in the lab trying things out. My PhD supervisor certainly did that. And, as a supervisor, I do that as well.

You should always make sure this is your PhD project and not his/hers. Your supervisor is a kind of mentor. S/he interferes with your work, makes suggestions, and at times shows some 'tough love' too. However, s/he should not spoil your project. You must be allowed to develop your way of doing things. You still follow the guidelines and perform your work as a good scientist would do. However, you should be aware that your supervisor is not a coach; s/he has not been trained to be a coach; his/her job does not require him/her to be a coach at all.

Finally, the path you want to take your project through must be down to you. You decide the most appropriate schedule and how to tune the effort you put in. As far as you deliver those agreed milestones with your supervisor, then it is down to you how you do it. It is good practice to keep your supervisor informed, so no surprise will ever upset anyone. Keep your supervisor also informed of your whereabouts. S/he is also responsible for your safety and general wellbeing.

My top tips for sailing through your PhD project

In this first chapter, we have looked at the basics ingredients of a cake you will prepare, bake, and then consume in future chapters. This is the fabulous and colorful cake of your PhD. Taking the analogy of a Formula 1 race, in this first chapter, we have seen the Saturday's qualifying sessions; they were short stints (corresponding to this chapter's sessions) in which we have measured ourselves against the racetrack (PhD framework). In the following chapter, we will witness the slightly more relaxed warm-up, which will end with the cars getting on the grid behind the checkered flag.

Before we get there, let's close this chapter with a non-exhaustive yet thoughtful list of tips I have gethered over the years by carefully analyzing a considerable number of PhD projects I managed. Many of these projects resulted in a positive outcome, with few being extremely satisfying. Unfortunately, very few left a sour taste in the mouth of all concerned, first among which the student.
Shall we dive in?

A more 'unique' than 'rare' catapult.
A PhD is like a catapult. You probably do not know yet that the most significant leap forward in our lives are not those we pursue by the everyday work based on incremental learning. The leaps ahead are achieved during those times in which we typically 'fight' an internal struggle. And it is by winning this internal struggle that we are visually propelled ahead in space and time. And you know what? The PhD provides you with just such a powerful catapult. That said, it is also important to point out that a catapult is loaded there but does not beacon you to step on it. It is your deliberate choice to climb on it and be fired higher up and further away.

You are your own master.
Your PhD will reveal this, probably for the first time in your life. You have the power to decide your own destiny. Even through difficulties, every human has at his/her disposal some critical choice to make. Making a choice and then realizing you need to change it is far better than taking no action at all. In the long run, by making choices, you will feel empowered, and you will always make fewer mistakes.

Reading and writing.
Strive to become a voracious reader. Because one day, you will automatically become a prolific writer. Read a lot of papers. Find some thesis, book chapters, and magazines to read from people around the World who did work in the same area. Read not only about your topic; also, read other genres. This will broaden your horizon. Writing will then become a natural and fluid process.

Distractions kill creativity and productivity.
Try to get work done before you spend precious time on online digressions and social activities. Early morning working hours are very productive because usually there are few distractions. Other people have not yet come to work or are engaged in coffee/tea sharing and internet searches.

Modulate your use of physical and mental energies.
Learn how to run and win a marathon instead of cashing in on a sprint. A PhD is a long shot marathon. A PhD is a great and unique experience. It should not be a full immersion only in work-related tasks. There is plenty of time for several other healthy and sound activities. If you do work mainly in front of a computer, remember to feed your body as well with physical activities. Regular short walks away from the screen can be extremely beneficial. Fresh air is even better for your

psychophysical wellbeing. Simple, various, and healthy food is also vital for withstanding the occasional stressful periods. Do not forget to take a couple of longer breaks (holidays) over the course of a year away from being connected all the time and thinking of work. Try not to take work-related activities on holidays. When you come back from a 'work-free' holiday, you will spring forward like a frog.

People around you matter.

Remember that you have a limited amount of energy and time at your disposal every day. Make fair use of it. Pay also attention to some toxic people around you. Most people are charming and even supportive, but a few are somewhat toxic. These poisonous people will literally drain your energies and steal your valuable time. If you have any of them around, probably it is wise considering keeping some distance from them.

Given many people around, you definitely have a superb chance to master your soft communication skills. For instance, learning to become a bit 'avoidant' is much better than being 'confrontational.' If you do not engage in confrontations, these sorts of people will look elsewhere for other opponents.

Relationship with the supervisor.

Your supervisor is a human being. As such s/he has work and private related issues. In principle, these issues should not interfere with you, but in practice, they do, to at least some extent. Your supervisor might know more than you at the beginning of your PhD, but you will later become the expert. Your success is his/her success. Remember that the supervisor is a kind of mentor. S/he is neither a coach nor a counselor. Therefore, s/he might 'tell' you what to do and even, from time to time, how to do things. You need to work on this relationship as it is key to the success of your project.

Set your own targets.

After an initial grooming period, figure out which targets you can set earlier on in your PhD. Some goals can be things such as a conference paper, which then might well turn into a journal paper. During the conference/journal paper preparation, you can volunteer to give talks to your peers in your department and get useful feedback. Setting intermediate targets is essential in a long-shot project such as a PhD. If carefully selected, these targets would help you break down such a big thing as a PhD project in small enough chunks that become more manageable.

Warm-up 2

A structured approach for sailing through a PhD project

This second chapter is like the warm-up of a Formula 1 race. And as such, it will equip you with the tools and especially the right mindset to face the competition keeping your head well above water. This chapter is more relaxed than the previous one. There were some jitters in Chapter 1, as we were not entirely sure of what to expect from a PhD project. In the warm-up, it is different. We do not need to grab the first spot on the grid in a limited amount of time. We are out with our car to inspect the track and get familiar with all those details we did not notice during the rush of Chapter 1.

Let's remind those who entered straight the race at the warm-up that this book is made of concise and inspiring sections, which allow PhD students to select those they deem essential for the particular part of the project they are in and neglect the rest. All chapters are self-contained, highly informative, and motivational. Each chapter is dedicated to a specific part of the PhD project. Chapter 2 covers from the last part of year one to around one-and-a-half-year mark.

Before you read any further, you should pay attention to the fact that a PhD is designed to be a MAJOR step up from an undergraduate degree course. In fact, in an undergraduate course, you will learn what others have done, by reading through textbooks and scientific papers. A PhD is an entirely different ball game. At the end of it, you will write a book, probably your first book ever. Plus, in most cases, you will not find much in textbooks about your specific project. Thus, you are really going ploughing virgin soil. That said, the knowledge you have accumulated so far, the curious and inquisitive mind of a child you definitely have, and your determination will allow you to sail through any water without fearing how deep that water is. The same is true for a sailor who confronts the sea and never worries much if it is 1, 10, 100, or 1,000 meters deep.

By faring well during a PhD, you will enter the realm of academia. This is harbored by a select bunch of people, many of whom are passionate about what they do. Some of them have a huge ego, which is probably why at times, student/supervisor relationship from looking like a smooth flowing river, this same river seems to enter a rough sea and, in very few cases, can even run on dry soil. In case you are not interested in academia after finishing your PhD, then the skills you have mastered will be equally important in your industrial career.

Did you know that you will inevitably become a good writer by writing scientific articles and especially your thesis? That is definitely true, no doubts about it. The key is to read a lot. The more you read, the more you will write. And, if you read a bit of everything out there (fiction, news magazines, history, etc.), your writing style will literally leap forward. In case you have saved some of your academic writing before you enter the PhD project, it is worth keeping a copy of those. At the end of your PhD, just compare the writing style you had reached with that before you started your PhD. It is not how much you have written. It is especially how much you have read that makes this difference.

I can't stop saying that you should never underestimate the benefit of maintaining a healthy lifestyle during the project's whole duration. A PhD lasts at least three years; this is a very long marathon. Calibrating how many energies you use along the way is vital for a smooth ride.

How to keep the initial mood lasting three years

Enrolling on a PhD project is typically not done because you have nothing else better to do. It is a choice. A deliberate choice for you to step up a notch. In Europe, this is even more true than in America. In America, holding a PhD can substantially boost your career options, and your income would be considerably higher with a PhD degree in your hands. Less so in Europe, where, apart from academia, of course, having a PhD only marginally boosts both the position you might get in a company and the salary. Obviously, things will change in the long run. Holding a PhD can also lead to landing top jobs in Europe as you advance in your career and become more experienced. This takes both time and devotion.

For this reason, it is far better to base your choice of seeking a PhD on a kind of urge you feel to prove your worth. You want to start by taking a problem, looking at it under a microscope lens, and finally become so familiar with it that you can not only talk proudly about it but also inspire others.

At times you are given a subject to start with. This was my case. I was introduced to a specific subject my supervisor was interested in. In other cases, the topic is not well defined. It is rather broad. In this case, it can be, at the same time, more exciting and daunting. In some other cases still, you propose the topic and then choose where to develop it. In all cases, you will always have to define the boundaries inside which you will operate. And this is an absolutely vital thing to do early on. We all want to explore more. If we were sent outside Earth's atmosphere, most of us would wonder in outer space forever. There is so much out there that we will find a new object to explore and experience every day. Well, it can quickly turn the same for your PhD project. Even if the page you start writing on has one top and two lateral borders that you will seldom breakthrough, the bottom edge is only a strange illusion. Keeping your PhD bounded is essential for two reasons.

First and foremost, if you define a program you can achieve, you are more likely to feel in control of it. A program that has become (also for your inputs) too ramified might well play against you; you can quickly lose focus and run out of time and energies. The second important consideration to make is that you should continue generating ideas but probably prioritize them according to a coherent plan that allows you to 'bang on your bucks.' Do not forget that there is time after getting your PhD to explore further those fancier or complicated ideas connected with your main topic. Actually, this is usually a natural progression and is an excellent way to write a research proposal for seeking some research grants after you have got your PhD degree.

One of the things I have seen with other students/researchers I managed and at times also with myself is that we humans not only deviate substantially from the original plan, but we even lose a lot of motivation in the process. Not to mention the drain of energies and valuable time throughout. Therefore, it is probably a good idea to remind ourselves, from time to time, the unique feelings we had when we first started the PhD. Those were most likely days in which we looked at the world from above, without being really arrogant. We perceived ourselves as being capable, had a tank full of energies, and felt that lot of time was in front of us. We could not fail back then at the start. This was what I also experienced.

How can a PhD student keep this upbeat frame of mind?
There are probably a lot of factors that have an essential contribution to this. However, I noticed with myself that keeping focus, cutting loose of limiting beliefs, and being ruthless with time are crucial elements to hold on to that

initial mindset that typically make PhD students so passionate and confident at the beginning of their program.

Then there is the crucial relationship with your supervisor. Some supervisors are really involved in the project; they might come to see you almost daily. Some others are more hands-off; they will see you once a week or bi-weekly or even once a month! You somehow need to manage this and understand where to get more support by networking with the right people.

One of the crucial things I understood earlier on is that every human needs to seek validation for what we do. This is paramount in the long run of a PhD project. From time to time, we need some good feedback reminding us that what we are doing is valuable. Validations are like mind rewards. They act as a 'chocolate treat' for our brain. The more genuine validations we get, the more we build confidence and keep ourselves upbeat. Strong-minded people can do a great job even without validations. Few can also excel in case of continuous invalidations from peers and those above them. But here we are digressing a little bit into psychology. I wanted to suggest that you should somehow catch that 'chocolate treat' from time to time. How do you do it? Well, if your supervisor is short of chocolates in his/her box, then share your work with good friends and peers. They might have some good chocolates for you. The following seems trivial, but it is not. Giving yourself a treat is also a way to validate the excellent work you do. I have learned how to self-validate regularly, as I hardly receive validations from others. And I even coped well with constant invalidations from a myriad of sources throughout my life.

Probably one right way to remind yourself of how you felt at the start of the PhD is to write down your feelings, sensation, and emotions during the first few weeks of your program. Like this, you can revisit them regularly as you progress in your PhD project and understand if any change needs to happen to bring you closer to the initial mental status. These days is even more powerful to record some short video clips in which you show how your mindset was at that particular time; this could be done at the very beginning of your PhD and throughout.

My last suggestion here is that whatever you do, do not overdo it. There is plenty of time to explore different avenues after you get your PhD. In the limited timespan of your PhD program, you want to avoid leaking energies and digressing. Stay focused. Keep distractions out. Be ruthless with time. And, of course, enjoy your valuable free time outside of work.

Cosimo Buffone

What is scientific research and how to conduct it

According to Merriam-Webster, the word 'Re – search' (https://www.merriam-webster.com/dictionary/research) means one of the following three things:

- 'Careful or diligent search;'
- An investigation aimed at discoveries or interpretation of facts;
- And the gathering of information on a specific topic.

A piece of research should aim at being ELEGANT, which means achieving its OBJECTIVES with the LEAST possible effort (basically minimizing time spent and avoiding waste of energies). We should adopt this as the basic principle of the research we will perform. This is a kind of principle and not a rule. This means that following principles leads a person farther away than obeying rules, as demonstrated in private relationships and social settings. Having digested this, now it is time to dive into some theory first and then some practical aspects of research through the lens of a motivated, curious, but probably still inexpert PhD student.

Doing scientific research follows a well-established method (at least in its broader terms) since Galileo Galilei proposed it in the seventeenth century. In reality, in ancient Greece, Aristotle had already pioneered the scientific method using the inductive-deductive approach. With inductions from observations, he proposed to infer general principles; and used deductions from those principles to check against further comments. Aristotle believed science could be demonstrated from principles, whereas Galileo was proposing the use of experiments as a powerful research tool (https://en.wikipedia.org/wiki/History_of_scientific_method).

What happened since then is that each of the steps of the research method has been defined more precisely and adapted to a large number of research fields, including those of social science.

You should be aware of the fact that there are two ways to investigate a problem. One way is to observe Nature directly. A second and far more conventional way is to reproduce Nature inside a laboratory. This is a massive simplification in itself. And there are real risks that the phenomenon to be investigated inside the lab has been conditioned somehow. On the other hand, a lab experiment allows for precise control of the same. This means the experimenter has a better chance of pinpointing the most likely explanation of what s/he measured during the experiments.

Another two distinctive aspects of research are related to the difference between qualitative and quantitative measurements as well as that between absolute and relative measurements. It is far more appropriate to have quantitative measurements that give a value less prone to questioning. However, there are cases in which quantitative measurements are not possible; a case in point is how hot or cold a person feels, to which we cannot assign a specific number. The current through a wire is known by measuring the number of charges (i.e., electrons) that pass through it in a given time; this is an absolute value. If we provide your lab's temperature in Celsius degree, that is a relative value compared to the absolute thermodynamic temperature measured in Kelvin.

The scientific method follows a sequence of steps, which are reported below:

1. Make an OBSERVATION of a phenomenon;
2. Ask yourself a QUESTION;
3. Put forward a HYPOTHESIS, which can be tested;
4. Generate a PREDICTION, which is based on the hypothesis proposed in step 3;

5. TEST the prediction of step 4;
6. In case the TEST shows that the PREDICTION matches the HYPOTHESIS, then STOP. Otherwise, generate other hypotheses or predictions and keep iterating UNTIL you are SATISFIED with the outcome.

We actually always perform such a sequential approach in our daily lives. We do not realize we are doing it or, as often happens, we get stuck between steps 4 and 5 of the previous list. For instance, we observe that there is a smell of burned wood. We ask if that is a concerning fire. We look around and having not seen flames, and we guess that the neighbors must be preparing for a barbecue. We reckon the fire must be under control. However, we forget to put this hypothesis/prediction under test. We could be listening for happy voices coming from the same direction as the smell. In case we do not hear them, we could also walk towards the place in a quest to pinpoint the exact location from where the smell comes from. If there are no voices, there is no smell of roasted meat, and the smoke seems to come from inside a building, then the whole original guess goes out of the window. In fact, a fire that starts inside an apartment where there are no people does not scream, does not smell of roasted meat, and thus it is certainly not a barbecue.

Now, let's give a more tangible example to demonstrate how this sequence of steps works in a typical case. We try turning on the laptop, and it does not work. The OBSERVATION would be that the laptop does not work. The QUESTION we could ask ourselves is: why the laptop does not work today? The following step is to formulate a HYPOTHESIS before we take any possible action. This hypothesis can be something like: maybe there is no electrical power connection. A possible PREDICTION is: if I put the plug inside the socket, it might work again. When I TEST the prediction just made, I realize it is NOT TRUE. At this point,

I am faced with either giving up or producing new hypotheses or predictions. A different PREDICTION could be to use an alternative socket to power on the laptop. When I test this other PREDICTION, I also get a negative outcome. Then instead of giving up, I can change the HYPOTHESIS and say that I might have a faulty battery. In this case, a possible PREDICTION would be: if I remove the battery and power the laptop directly from the mains, then it might work. I TEST this PREDICTION, and the answer is again negative. At this point, not having other means to test the electrical connections, I can conclude with reasonable accuracy that the laptop itself must have an electrical fault. And with this I have kind of closed my investigation by having reached a negative but SATISFACTORY outcome, given the tools at my disposal.

If we humans would apply this iterative approach of the scientific method to all spheres of our lives, we would probably avoid a lot of distress to others and ourselves too. For instance, when we meet a difficult person, we have already made the OBSERVATION: this person is difficult. Then some of us might want to understand more, and we ask (i.e., QUESTION) ourselves (consciously or unconsciously): why this person behaves like this? If we do, then after that, we should also formulate a HYPOTHESIS; instead, we might well rush to conclude that this person is an aggressor. By having curtailed the process at step 3 of the above list, we have no means to finish the loop and test all possible hypotheses and predictions we could have generated. For instance, we could have said: this person seems distressed (HYPOTHESIS) because maybe he does not behave rationally (PREDICTION). Following from this, I could TEST this prediction with a set of thoughtful questions and then conclude.

It could well be that a problem does not have a solution. Maybe there are limits with the nature of the experiment itself, the testing equipment's capabilities, or the experimenter's limitations. All of these factors, or any combination thereof, would lead to NO SOLUTION for the problem. In this case, the experimenter is SATISFIED to have investigated all possible scenarios. In such cases, the experimental campaign can be considered as closed.

Even before applying the scientific method described with the six steps mentioned above, we should ask ourselves some more general and philosophical questions. Let's look into them one at a time. The first is the ONTOLOGICAL question in which we ask ourselves if the 'reality' we observe is real, or it is a mental construction we make because of our limitations. For instance, our eyes can only see a small portion of the whole electromagnetic field; therefore, what we 'see' is not what is 'out there.' The second is the EPISTEMOLOGICAL question in which we should ask ourselves if the reality under investigation is understandable. What is the relationship between the researcher and the case under investigation? The third is the METHODOLOGICAL question in which we ask ourselves how we can unveil reality. How can we be sure that our chosen methods to investigate the truth can satisfy the objectives we have set? The fourth point groups the TECHNICAL and OPERATIONAL dimensions with which we decide the techniques and instruments we want to use to get a valid and accurate result. The fifth is an AXIOLOGICAL question that relates to ethics. A typical case of this is when living organisms or body parts are used in an experiment. Even when some people are tested for an extended period or an astronaut goes up in space for prolonged exposure to damaging cosmic radiation, ethical questions must be addressed before the study commences.

Having given a general view of the scientific method and analyzed some even more fundamental questions the experimenter should address, it is time to get into the nitty-gritty of performing research in the lab. In the following, we will elaborate more about the core of the scientific method giving some specific suggestions on how to go about it.

Scientific research stems from some sort of intuition. Typically, a researcher working on a specific topic has an intuition (most of the time, by observing something peculiar), and the quest becomes how to prove or disprove that intuition. This is the real core of scientific research. And this is also what you should aim for. How can you start moving along this path? Well, I give you an example of how I started walking on this path. My supervisor introduced me to the topic of my PhD when one day soon after I joined him, he asked me to do the following: take a small transparent tube, fill with a mixture of alcohol and some tiny particles, then place this tube under an old microscope of the '60s and, as per a magic trick, all was revealed. What I saw under the microscope was simply amazing. Something was moving and I did not provide any power from the outside of the tube for this vigorous movement to happen inside that tiny quantity of liquid that partially filled the tube. I could not believe what my eyes were seeing! Without me knowing it, my supervisor had planted in my mind the right seed. He had stimulated my curiosity. A seed that kept growing throughout those two years and ten months before I sat my thesis defense. No. That was a massive understatement. I am still partially working on that subject to these days, nearly twenty years after seeing those little vortices inside that transparent capillary tube filled with ethanol and some very minute aluminum particles. How amazing is that?

Once the curiosity has been sparked with planting a seed and the excitement of having started a PhD is high, this is the perfect mix to move forward and get your hands dirty. In case you are going to work in the lab, start learning safety procedures such as how to safely operate equipment, especially the characteristics of the equipment you will use to take measurements. Each measuring tool is based on a physical principle and is used to measure a parameter which is the product of yet another physical principle. Therefore, you need to get acquainted with how the instrument works and which are its limits. This process will give you the device accuracy and sensitivity. At this point, establish the minimum and maximum values of the parameter that you want to measure with the instrument you have at your disposal. In case you have to buy a new device, you still need to assess the range of values of the parameter you want to measure. Then you will try to purchase or use the instrument you already have in the lab towards its top scale. This way, you minimize measuring errors because the closer the value of the parameter you want to measure is to the bottom scale of the instrument, the larger the error you will make. Let's clarify this point with an example: if we want to measure a bag of 1 kg of sugar, we can either take a kitchen scale with a maximum range of 2.5 kg or a scale measuring people weight with a maximum range of 150 kg. If both scales have a systematic error of 1%, placing the 1 kg bag of sugar on the kitchen scale leads to a potential maximum error of 25 g; instead, on the larger scale, we can have an error of 1.5 kg, which is larger than the weight of the bag of sugar itself!

Having reached this point, you should start performing some preliminary tests even if you are using a kind of 'improvised' test article. Gain some knowledge on your experiment. By doing so, you will learn which are the parameters that control your experiment. They can be things such as temperature, pressure, humidity, heat load, volume, surface, linear dimension, etc. Once this list is compiled, you should also run some preliminary tests assessing which of these parameters are more critical for your experiment. In some cases, the influence of one or more parameters is so small compared to the others that it does not make any sense to spend any quality time to perform an extensive experimental campaign on them.

There are a lot of potential biases in research, as in any other field. This is even true in private matters, not excluding personal interactions. Therefore, it is a good idea to think about how to rule out some of these biases. You, as a researcher, are one of the most challenging biases for your experiment. This is because overall, we humans are 'optimistic.' Thus, we jump to conclusions as soon as we see in our investigation something of potential interest. And before we know it, we have formed in our mind a rather 'rigid' picture of what we might have just perceived to be a real thing. Our brain is a champion at building something out of very thin air. Our brain cannot store all the information that reaches it, so its most powerful trait is to paint pictures out of tiny details. Did you know that storing information about all the senses we use when wondering for just a couple of hours in a picturesque park would literally use the entire memory of our brain? For this reason, our brain stores very little of what our senses transmit to it. So, how does it play back then? Well, it starts from the small details he has fine-tuned into when in recording mode and then continues reconstructing all that might have been around it. Let's give an example to show how it works. I went skiing with my friends last year and now I am trying to recollect what was in front of us at the resting place during our break when a skier hit my best friend. Indeed I remember my friend in pain rather well: where he was standing, what color jacket he was wearing, if we walked to get help or if the accident was so severe that an ambulance was called. But most likely, I would not remember things such as how many people were there, how much snow was around, and if it was sunny that day. Our brain starts filling these voids. It might put a lot of snow in the reconstructed picture because we were somewhat happy about skiing on the slopes until the accident took place. It might put lots of people in the frame because we usually took a break around 2 pm when people were still having lunch or enjoying a coffee/hot chocolate. If it looked so good, then the sun must have been shining too, as a sunny day brings a slime in the face of everyone resting outside. You see! Our brain is a MASTER at reconstructing things, all in a blink of an eye. For this reason, you need to make sure you are not introducing the most entrenched biases in your experiment. How do we avoid that, then?

I tend to do the following whenever I can. I repeat the same experiment several times and randomly for several days. Then I ask a colleague (even one of my students is ok) to repeat the same experiment and give me her/his impressions on what s/he observes. If the colleague/student sees more or less what I saw, then my brain did not fool me this time. You can also bring your supervisor to the lab and ask him/her to comment on what you are seeing. Maybe your supervisor is intrigued enough that s/he will run the experiment to understand better what is happening and why your experiment behaves as it does.

Once the phenomenon has been 'captured on camera,' so to speak, it is time to dedicate a few good days to face all possible systematic errors. These sorts of errors are easy to pinpoint, and it is worth removing them outright. How? Let's assume you suspect that ambient conditions play a massive role in your experiment. All you have to do is to run the experiment at different times during the day. Ensure you have a reasonably accurate measurement of the outside temperature, pressure, and humidity (if you are working with water or any item that is sensitive to water content in the atmosphere). Check also weather forecast sites, as they give relatively accurate measurements of ambient conditions in your city. Then measure the temperature, pressure, and humidity inside your lab. Run the tests, say, around 7 am (when most likely nobody else is in the lab). Repeat it around 10 am, sometimes around 1 pm, around 4 pm, and finally around 7 pm and record the values all the critical parameters controlling your experiment. Do this for a few days. In the end, you will have a matrix of values for the key parameters you measured for your study, and you can easily spot if there is any significant influence of ambient conditions on them. In case the influence of ambient conditions is important, you need to isolate your test article from the varying ambient conditions. To address this issue, you need to develop a proper strategy which depends on your test article (dimensions, shape, volume, mass, materials), the parameters to be measured, and how sensitive they are to ambient conditions.

One paramount tip is to keep a detailed lab book of your experiments. You start a new page every day (put down the experiment's date and time) and record the ambient conditions and the values of all parameters you measured. A sensible approach these days is to take pictures of the experimental setup as you are building it. These pictures can be precious when you write both scientific articles and, of course, your thesis. Not to mention presentations for meetings, conferences, and even your thesis' defense.

This preliminary exploration we just described might last a few good months. You will gain valuable insight into things such as: how many parameters are there that you should vary; how long it takes for you to complete a single experimental run; and, how long it would take to map the full matrix of parameters by running all necessary experiments. This is an essential piece of information as it gives you the ability to plan for the experimental campaign. What I have done at this stage was to devise a plan for how many sets of different experiments I could run for a particular combination of parameters to get enough data for producing one scientific paper. This was a critical decision I made on my own. And it helped me in so many ways afterward. Let's comment on some of the advantages that this approach brought. Firstly, by finishing a set of experiments and then writing a manuscript on it allowed me to get that so important reward for my brain that resulted in a renewing boost to carry on more motivated than before. Then comes the fact that by writing a manuscript, I had to make schemes for the experimental setups, modify pictures I took, and of course, post-process raw data I recorded. This resulted in me having a sizable part of my thesis already written while submitting manuscripts for journal publication. The third and last advantage of slicing the work this way is that I was not put off at all about many tests I had to do. Crucially, by post-processing the data I was taking as I went along, I ran fewer risks later of forgetting details of what I did. If I had waited even a single year to write a manuscript after I finished a set of experiments, the chances are that I would have forgotten some details about it. Let alone if I would have done this at the very end of the whole experimental campaign, as many, but not all, PhD students do. My supervisor was also pleased and supportive of this approach of mine. He benefitted so much from it that my PhD thesis (according to his own words), which reflects this approach I took, became a template for all of his subsequent PhD students.

Do not forget to perform the error analysis. This is of paramount importance to understand of which quality is the data you took. There are a few papers I liked about how to perform the error analysis, and below I suggest two of them that I have used over the years:

Kline, S. J. and McClintock, F. A. (1953). Describing the uncertainties in single sample experiments. Mechanical Engineering, pages 3–8.

Moffat, R. J. (1988). Describing the uncertainties in experimental results. Experimental Thermal and Fluid Science, 1:3–17.

Error analysis is a piece of science on its own. It is somewhat complicated, and one can acquire valuable knowledge if studied thoroughly. We are NOT going to do it here, as it would take a large portion of this book. If you start digging from the two references given above, then you can quickly learn a lot about error analysis. Before we proceed further, let's make a primary distinction between ERROR and MISTAKE. They are not the same thing. An ERROR is something you end up doing because you did not know how to do it. Instead, a MISTAKE is something you did when you knew how to do it, but you simply failed it for some reason. Therefore, a mistake is much simpler to rectify than an error of which you might even not be aware of. Mistakes are similar to certain types of systematic errors that can be ruled out of your experiment with a bit of patience. Systematic errors are associated with worn-out instruments, incorrectly calibrated devices, and experimenters consistently taking incorrect readings. Errors are also random, such as noise and vibrations, which have no specific pattern associated with them. Random errors are typically unavoidable and cannot be replicated. For this book's purpose, in what following of this chapter, we will refer only to systematic errors.

When you step on the error analysis, you are practically at the evaluation stage of what you have collected as data. And you are trying to show how good are the results you are presenting. In general, for reducing the error you make in measuring a parameter, you can minimize the instrument's errors and the errors you make as an operator of the device. Unless the apparatus is 'homemade,' you have little chance to minimize the instrument's error; the only thing you should regularly perform is a calibration of the instrument. This is because each device will drift over time (even if not used), and it must be recalibrated. If the instrument is delicate and expensive, it is probably wise to ask the manufacturer for calibration; they will typically deliver also a calibration certificate. The errors made by you using the instrument to measure a parameter are usually minimized by increasing the number of repeat measurements, wherever possible maintaining the same measurement procedure. In case you are not convinced, you can also ask a colleague to measure the same parameter several times and compare it with your measurements; this will show if there is and how significant is the dependency of the operator's error. Now, how many repeat measurements should be done? This is a tricky question. In theory, statistics show that the more repetition you make, the more accurate the measurements are. The problem is that this is not feasible most of the time. Inserting the instrument inside the experiment can change the value of the parameter to be measured, and if this operation is repeated many times, it can produce somewhat inaccurate results. In other cases, the experiment should be set from scratch altogether after every time the instrument is inserted in the experimental domain. Even in those cases where the apparatus is non-contact, the experiment itself can have a non-stationary nature, and therefore you can only take one sample of the measurement.

Thus, what do we do in such cases? The solution is to repeat the experiment at least three or possibly five times. If the experiment is stationary and the measurement operation does not disrupt the physics, then you can take three to five measurements without starting the test again from scratch. In the case of an unsteady experiment, the same should be repeated from scratch three to five times, and particular care should be given at the sampling time. Then use the approach described in (Kline and McClintock, 1953) to derive the average and the standard deviation. This latter indicates how accurate the measurements are; small values of standard deviation mean that there is little spread of the data collected around the average value.

At times, an underestimated aspect is cleaning the experimental cell after each run or set of runs. Sometimes this is done after a few weeks or months of tests. It depends on the experiment and how easily it gets contaminated by the environment. You should assess this aspect at the beginning of your experimental campaign to ensure the data you collect over time is consistent. There are often indirect ways to tell if what is inside the experimental cell has changed noticeably. For instance, in a condensation experiment, typically, any air inside the experimental cell is non-wanted, and therefore its presence would significantly affect the data collected. One way to know if air has made its way inside the test cell is to measure pressure at a set operating temperature. When the value of pressure inside the cell (say when the cell is not working) is above a certain threshold, it means air has entered the cell, and the cell should be vented before a new experiment is carried out. Be aware that touching surfaces with your fingers will leave grease on them, which could affect the measurements. Use gloves when you suspect this is an issue. In some more delicate experiments, you should also wear a mask to avoid contamination of the specimens with your breath. In surface science studies, the test can be run only once, and then proper cleaning or even replacement of the sample is needed. This is because, in surface science, both phenomena and measurements are very susceptible to contaminations and aging.

We should make a short stop here talking about a delicate subject. We will give only some general principles here. It would help if you got trained adequately by your university before entering the lab and performing experiments there. Your safety, the safety of others inside the lab, and the building are PARAMOUNT. Sometimes you work with flammable fluids. Some other times you might be using pressurized gasses. Heated plates and wires can also cause damage to you, to others, and to property. You might even be required to use lasers. In all such cases, you should get familiar with the safety instructions in your university. Always wear a lab coat and protective glasses. Take special care when handling naked flames. Use a fume cupboard when handling liquids and gasses. Be sure you know which substance you are handling and how harmful it can be to you and others around you. Read the manufacturer label and ask technicians how to handle it and where to store it. For using lasers, typically, you will be sent to a particular safety course because lasers have the power to blind you and others even when the laser beam is not directly pointed at the eyes. The best thing to do is to ask your supervisor about the safety courses your university runs and how to sign up for them. Make safety the number one priority in your lab. Keep your lab tidy and clean. This will avoid accidental spillage, falls, and fires. Get accustomed to the safety exits around your lab and how to report an accident. DO NOT TRY TO FIX an accident yourself, especially if it is serious, such as a fire, significant leakage, or an injured colleague. You might do more harm than good. Seek help using the phone and immediately inform your supervisor and the school manager. Then put yourself in a safe place, possibly outside of the building, and remember to close the door and the windows behind you when you leave the area affected. Once the accident has been cleared, you should note in the lab safety book and provide valuable information to the university safety personnel. Such reporting is critical also to put in place procedures to avoid that similar cases repeat. You should not bring food and drinking liquids inside the lab. These could get poisoned, or similar containers having harmful content inside can be mistaken for being safe, and someone (including yourself) can get seriously harmed by unintentionally swallowing the contents.

After this short spell on safety, now we can rejoin our main flow of technical ideas. At this point, you have collected all the data for your manuscript, and now you want to produce some graphs to embed inside the text. You would like to be in a position where you have a lot of data to choose from, kind of going 'cherry-picking' as this gives you more freedom and shows that you have indeed performed a sizable number of tests. Now it is time to choose the type of software that allows you to make compelling and eye-catching graphs/plots. In science circles, using Excel to plot data looks somewhat awkward and primitive; it is a far too simple software package for plotting, and you have little control over the dimensions of each line, text, labels, etc. As you will be producing many graphs/plots, it is probably a good idea to either learn how to use some free plotting tools found on the web or buy a professional plotting tool. Because graphs/plots are inserted inside the text and then re-sized, make sure that the small fonts can be read. Also, make an appropriate selection of lines, patterns, and colors. Using too thin lines is not a good idea, and using light colors such as green and yellow is not advisable because when people print your paper, these colors will not print very well.

If you reached this point, you are a step away from writing your paper. And this is a different topic described in detail in one of the sessions of the next chapter.

There are a few concluding remarks of this section. The first remark is that while you select the data to be included in the manuscript, do not forget that the data you just discarded could at least go in your thesis, and it is probably a good idea also to process them now. Maybe the scrapped data could be enriched and form a second separate manuscript later on. The second aspect is that I tend to keep a list of ideas that I generate while performing experiments, post-processing the data, and write a manuscript for a particular topic. These ideas could well become offspring or, at the very least different branches of the same growing tree. The last remark is that science is not perfect, and you should not strive for perfection either. You should aim at generating fascinating ideas or very peculiar ways to look at an old problem. You should also aim at being very convincing with the data you present, how you present it, and the explanation you bring to justify what you have observed.

See if you can get comfortable with the thought that you have been tasked to unveil Nature, which is contained inside your test article. And that you are a kind of a curious and inquisitive explorer who does not become part of the story itself. You will tell the story, but you are not part of it, and, very importantly, you have not deliberately influenced it.

Tips for sustaining body/mind during a three years long marathon

Probably the most important thing you should remind yourself during your PhD is the following: It was, by and large, my own choice. A PhD project typically pays a salary far less than a fresh graduate job in science and engineering. Therefore, you should have been ready to 'rock and roll' and enjoy as much as possible the precious thinking time you also have during these three years.

There is a quote by American lawyer and politician Frank A. Clark which says: 'If you find a path with no obstacles, it probably doesn't lead anywhere.' The same goes for PhD projects. Another thing we all forget about is that 'work' comes from the Greek word 'εργον,' the etymology of which basically means the 'outcome of a worker who accomplishes something.' This is a crucial aspect of work in general. It is about accomplishing something. This Greek word has an even deeper meaning for you, boys and girls, who have decided to take the word 'εργον' to an entirely new level. You have basically challenged that, and probably without knowing it, with the PhD you are striving to achieve more than to accomplish. And here lies a possible pitfall. The sooner you learn about it, the more these three years spent for your PhD will be very valuable to yourself and the wider community.

I should remind you that our governments inject many resources into the educational system with the deliberate intent to create better people by alphabetizing kids. Then helping young adults develop the right attitude of 'learning how to learn.' And finally, our educational system also contributes reinforcing the scaffolding of our personalities on which most of our lives as humans depend. Once you get out of education, you should be equipped with the tools to do very well for yourself and, at the very least, not damage others. In many cases, you can also help others who will be your colleagues or subordinates and, in some cases, even help managers in the process.

I suggest you read this short article from Marc Prensky (http://marcprensky.com/wp-content/uploads/2013/04/Prensky-Achievement-vs-Accomplishment-FINAL.pdf) about the difference between 'achieving' and 'accomplishing.' I believe you can do both. You have at least one supervisor who helps you; what you achieve, s/he achieves, and both accomplish. Then you will automatically accomplish for your university as well, for your project's funding body, and the country as a whole. Therefore, the PhD is a perfect example of where your endeavors merge exceptionally well with the strive of many others around you, and at the end of your project, you can be proud of all you did. At that very moment, all the hurdles you overtook might look small and insignificant as well. If I were you, I would keep this point in mind throughout the PhD project.

After this injection of motivation, it is essential to note that other aspects play a massive role in how easy or difficult we find the ride. There are bumps, potholes, mud, and even some STOP signs along the way. How do we prepare ourselves to deal with all of these obstacles?

While the specifics are left to you, some general suggestions can still be given. I would start reading. Reading allows you to literally 'pick up' the writer's brain. Read not only scientific articles but also books, PhD thesis, and websites. For the websites you read, you should check who wrote them, and if they belong to a trustworthy organization. Make a note of the URL and the time you accessed the site because it can be moved or even removed altogether from the net. If you deem the website you access is really important for you, other than saving the hyperlink, do make some screenshots of the contents or even print them.

The following suggestion I have is to try and stick to a routine. Get to work around the same time and schedule regular breaks. This should not be that difficult as usually you are pooled with other PhD students around your department. Try and eat healthy food and drink plenty of fluids, better if just water. I recommend limiting coffee intake to one or maximum two per day; why not try green or jasmine tea (much better if you buy the leaves and brew the tea and why not share it with your colleagues/friends). Tea is antioxidant and basic, whereas coffee is acid and will upset your stomach as well as your nervous system. Tea has the same boosting effect as coffee, without the drawbacks of coffee. The result of coffee is like a quick shot; it lasts only a few minutes. If you drink a glass of water after taking a coffee, its effect can be prolonged. Instead, the boosting effect of tea spans over a very long time, and you will feel much more hydrated as well. Restaurants inside the university campus offer a large variety of vegetables and some fruits as well. I would still consume meat or fish three to four times per week. In case your diet has particular connotations, then make sure your iron and protein intake is appropriate for the kind of activities you are involved in. Doing some sport is excellent but requires you to consider if your diet needs to be molded along with it. Nowadays, very detailed information about foods with even weekly plans is at the click of a mouse. Thus, there is no need to be specific here for such widely available and broadly accurate information. The only aspect I would stress is that the sooner you get into healthy eating habits, the better it is for your overall health. Finally, I suggest keeping an organized lifestyle also at home. And if possible, be asleep between 11 pm and 2 am as this is typically the timeslot of the night when most humans experience very deep and restoring sleep.

The next point is about taking work home. I only did it for a paper that was outside of my PhD core work. I could not find quality time at work to write some sections of this paper, and I decided to take it home. I do not think you need to take work home. It is a good idea to have a sort of mental separation between work and home. They are NOT the same thing. These two places do NOT mean the same thing to you. Why should you mix them in your mind? You can always stay a bit longer at work and get your task finished there. Typically, PhD rooms are pretty quiet; as a visitor, I have been inside one of them recently for a few months, and it was pretty much tranquil.

You should develop new interests as you also foster new friendships. If you start from the first year, then it can become a routine. If you do work in the lab, then your hands are rather busy touching different objects, and typically, people cope better than those sitting in front of a PC for the entire duration of their PhD project. In case you have a numerical or analytical PhD project, it is probably a good idea to develop some interests in which your body moves, and possibly you also use your hands holding or touching objects. This approach is precious to your brain, and you should do it a few good times per week. For those who remain sat most of the time, regular walking breaks are a NECESSITY. Otherwise, your muscles will stifle up, and you will soon feel tense and contracted. Adjust also the look of the space around your desk. Maybe put a small plant and some cute and colorful pictures around. Regularly open the window for letting fresh air in the room. I tend to use colorful posters and photographs, as well as some mugs. Then I keep plenty of stationery around and clean the desk space regularly as bacteria will otherwise proliferate. Every few months, I scan through the paper I have accumulated on the desk and decide what to do with it: keep it in a storage place or dump it. I do not want things piling up in front of my eyes because I feel heavier and heavier as the mountain's size grows.

How planning remains key to long term success

In this section, we are going to look at two examples of planning. The first example is straightforward as it is related to a single topic, and most of the activities are down to the researcher performing them. The second example is much more complex, and most of the events are outside the researcher's full control. Most likely, in your PhD project, your case will fall somewhere between these two extreme examples.

The first case requires good work habits and some degree of flexibility. The second is an entirely different beast altogether. It requires a lot of strategic thinking, the deployment of many different tactics, a lot of self-drive, some pretty good gut, and of course, some luck as well.

Shall we begin?

We will use Excel to make a time plan and show different activities. If any change to the original plan is needed, we will update it as we go along. Planning should not be used in trivial cases where activities span short periods and require little effort. For instance, if I have to plan for a new experimental investigation in which I want to explore some ideas using what I already have in the lab, careful planning might not help much. Actually, it can fall into the category of 'micro-managing', which might waste precious time and effort that could be used more productively. Let's have a closer look at the first of these two projects. First, there is some reading to be done so I can be sure to investigate new ideas on a scientific topic. After this, I design the test facility. I would need to gather or buy some new disposables for the tests. Later, I would set up the test facility using existing equipment (some of which I might adapt as a first pass). And finally, I would run the exploratory tests and see if I can spot any exciting features that I might want to record the events. At this point, the short exploratory project is concluded. Of course, in both cases (positive or negative outcome), I can decide to either conceive some other test or develop a testing procedure for a more in-depth investigation. Still, these are all subsequent tasks probably part of a new project. Usually, these sorts of exploratory projects have a short duration; in my personal experience, they lasted at most a few weeks. They are sequential, and, to a large extend, I have almost complete control over them. In fact, if I am not the only person working on them, I tend to work very closely in the lab with the other people involved, which I have cherry-picked beforehand.

The figure below shows the plan for this small project with five tasks and spanning sixteen weeks. As can be seen, it is sequential. The grey boxes represent the span of each activity. I am the only owner of all tasks, meaning that I am responsible for their execution. You can also spot that I have factored some slag between tasks 3 and 4. This is good practice where there is some uncertainty on when activities can start and finish. Tasks 1 and 2 are under my complete control.

The risk of delay here is minimal. But task 3 requires procuring parts that transfer some of the control to third parties (usually outside companies that I use to buy components from); in such case, it is wise to forecast some possible delay according to what the vendors have given as lead time for delivery. Making these sorts of planning and then following them regularly is also very useful to build confidence in predicting how long a task can last, delivering the overall project in time, and, if it was a project in industry, also on budget. Yes, because software packages used for planning projects also can enter costs. You might have noticed that I did not put any milestone in this planning. The project is short, sequential, and mainly down to me. For such types of projects, I prefer not to use milestones. The only real milestone is the achievement of the project's end goal.

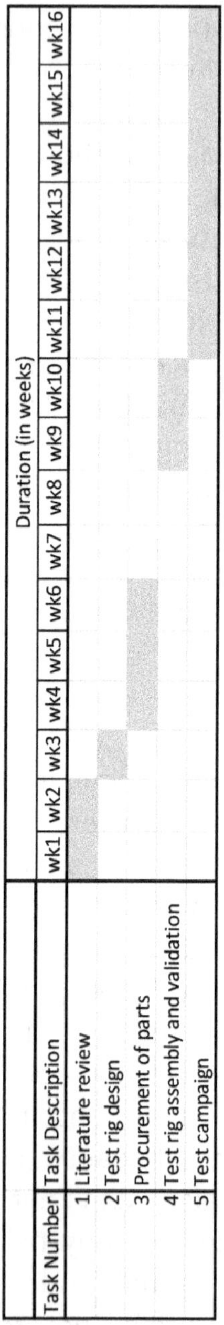

Task Number	Task Description	Duration (in weeks)															
		wk1	wk2	wk3	wk4	wk5	wk6	wk7	wk8	wk9	wk10	wk11	wk12	wk13	wk14	wk15	wk16
1	Literature review																
2	Test rig design																
3	Procurement of parts																
4	Test rig assembly and validation																
5	Test campaign																

I should still track the project's progress at regular intervals to spot possible issues as it unfolds. The figure above shows the status of the project at week 7. The black bar represents the actual progress of each activity.

Task Number	Task Description	Duration (in weeks)															
		wk1	wk2	wk3	wk4	wk5	wk6	wk7	wk8	wk9	wk10	wk11	wk12	wk13	wk14	wk15	wk16
1	Literature review	█	█														
2	Test rig design			█													
3	Procurement of parts				█	█	█	█									
4	Test rig assembly and validation									█	█						
5	Test campaign											█	█	█	█	█	█

At week seven, we record a delay in task 3 of one week, which is less than the predicted possible maximum delay of two weeks in the procurement of parts. Now that we have one free week available, we can decide how to use it most effectively. We can take this week off and relax or bring the plan forward by one week. It really depends on our judgment. I typically have some decent breaks after four or five months of solid work. For the whole project duration, we are at the lower end of such interval, so I decide to continue working and pushing the project forward by one week. At the end of the project, I have the new status reported in the figure below.

The final executed plan shows that also, task 4 took longer than predicted. However, the planned slag of two weeks allowed me to finish the project on time without reverting to extra-long hours.

A completely different ball game is a long and complicated project that includes several individuals inside and outside of the organization. In such a case, planning is of paramount importance. Monitoring how the project is doing is even more essential. These two aspects (planning and monitoring) allow the project manager to think strategically about which steps s/he needs to take to solve issues encountered along the way on some tasks or even face completely unexpected problems that will require the planning of new activities.

We are going to take another example from an overly complicated work experience of mine. The details of such a case are much harsher than described below. You won't be facing such stiff issues. Still, I wanted to show you how dynamically planning can be and how flexible a researcher must be to achieve the final goal, regardless of how many impediments are found along the way and how difficult some of them might be.

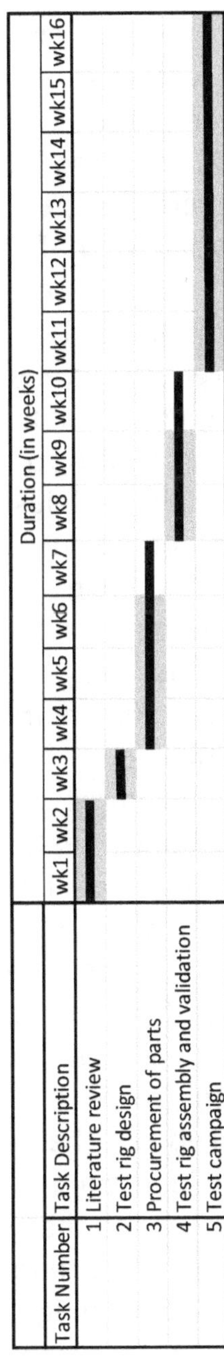

Task Number	Task Description	Duration (in weeks)															
		wk1	wk2	wk3	wk4	wk5	wk6	wk7	wk8	wk9	wk10	wk11	wk12	wk13	wk14	wk15	wk16
1	Literature review																
2	Test rig design																
3	Procurement of parts																
4	Test rig assembly and validation																
5	Test campaign																

In the following, I will use a narration approach for you to grasp the broader context in which the plan was molded, continuously changed, and executed to almost perfection, given the perilous circumstances in which I found myself to operate in just less than six months into the project.

This three-year project's principal goal was to publish several papers and help the locals establish a research reputation. The number of papers was either four in the first category of the journal list defined by that country, or two in the first and four and the second category, or two in the first category and bringing 120,000 Euro in total funding. While this sort of target would seem rather achievable at first sight, it had several potential pitfalls. Before accepting the project, I went to pay a visit to the new university to meet the people, see the lab facilities, and understand in a few days if I could have settled in such a different cultural and social environment. Of course, as in any visit, the host tries hard to impress by putting you in the best accommodation facilities around (it is only for a few days, anyway). Additionally, your host puts a friendly show for you to see and get excited about.

While I was unimpressed about some of the all-inclusive university campus features and what I saw of the students' life during those few days of my first visit, my main concern was the lab. The lab was where I should have spent a good part of those three years to achieve my primary target. Upon visiting the lab, some master students were performing an experiment that I had never seen before. They had visibly cleaned the place and were going to demonstrate the project they worked on: the spreading of liquid lenses on liquid substrates. While I did not know anything about this topic, I noticed that one of the young ladies had deposited several drops (probably more than six) on the liquid substrate, and each time she was saying that perhaps with the next drop, we would have seen a lens forming. I was puzzled at this. Eventually, after a few more drops deposited carefully with the aid of a handheld microsyringe with a bend and long stainless-steel needle, the student managed to have a very thin and wide lens. This lens shrank very quickly (in a matter of seconds), evaporating into the surrounding air. Then they showed me how they used software to treat the images acquired by a CMOS camera to get the temporal evolution of the lens radius. I was impressed with this part of their post-processing, which they had developed rather well. At this point, I started asking some technical questions, and neither they nor the more senior professors around were able to answer adequately. When the professors moved a little away from the experimental cell, I asked the students how long they were working on that project. They said it was about one and a half years.

The rest of the visit went well. I was taken out for a meal and then wondering around that megacity. The professors involved in this project talked about a massive shopping spree they were planning because they were close to secure some considerable funding for a new lab. When I returned to the hotel, I started processing in my mind what I had seen and heard. I went through my feelings, my intuitions, and of course, the relaxed chats with students and professors. I quickly concluded that because my work would have been lab-based and that the lab I had seen was the only one I could rely on, I had to have a plan B. Additionally, this plan B was even more critical because I would have had only Master students there; these students had to take full-time courses during the first of their three years of stay. When I eventually returned to my usual workplace in Europe, I started thinking about what I could have done to start the new job on the front foot (this was plan B). In just over five weeks, I started a vast experimental campaign on four projects related to evaporation, one of which related to the liquid lens I saw in that lab. On this project on liquid lenses, I felt like a hyena, seizing the prey the predators did not learn how to eat. I had to read some references about three of these related projects and quickly perform tests to gather enough data. It was a very intense five weeks but really rewarding, as I was planning ahead of a big jump with closed eyes into the unknown. And I found this rather exciting instead of being frightening.

While this happened, I received the paperwork for the new job, and after many iterations, we signed it. I started producing all the documentation (including visa) to settle in this new country, sometimes in June of that year.

After I landed in the new country, I started interacting with people. I had to solve many issues relating to the flat (which was not ready when I arrived and then was given to me as almost bare walls). There were also issues with the paperwork, adapting to the food, finding a water filtration system to use tap water that is not sanitized there. Then, just over one month from the start date, a problem ensued with the visa, and I had to go back to my home country to solve it. By the middle of August, when I arrived back at the new workplace, I noticed students coming later and taking it with some philosophy. Almost everybody seemed nice, but this later revealed to be their cultural approach to foreign, where locals do not want to appear less than foreign, and therefore pretty rarely they say 'No.' During the last leg of August, I made a plan for my work and included in this plan, the students who were assigned to me. Some had been there for two years, and some others were about to start. The program looked like the one in the figure below. Let's call this Plan A0. The duration of the program is expressed in Months (M1, M2, M3, etc.). The blue column would be the holidays or time away from the university. As we will see with the new subsequent planning, this 'time off' will constitute a large chunk of the project. While I was not happy with it, I had to either simply comply or be 'forced to comply' with my new employer's philosophy. The first plan (Plan A0) spanned only a few months as I wanted to keep it light and 'taste the water.'

I wanted to immerse myself in the new culture and started interacting a lot with students around. Hanging out for drinking, having some delicious meals together, and with two of the most audacious of them, we went by bicycle to the sea (return trip of around 120 km in just over 12 hours). That was one of the best experiences I had with students in all countries I had been to. These details seem irrelevant at first sight. But they are not, because for me to succeed, I had to bond with local students and make them feel, somehow, I was on their side. And if I was not entirely on their side, at least I was prepared to be treated as I was. I showed all people around my keen interest in learning their culture, history, and even their language; despite being so different from the ones I could speak and write before arriving there.

I knew about my Plan B, but I did not pull it out as soon as I encountered issues. This could have been taken as an insult by the locals. Therefore, I started thinking aloud how to get some help from the outside to kick-start a few other projects. I proposed some new ideas and then began getting in touch with people I knew from Europe who could have lent a substantial hand. What happened next would have taken me almost one more year to grasp fully. We were now at the start of November and I started feeling some pressure to kick-start programs the way I conceived them, after having communicated widely and agreed upon with students and my superiors. For one of the external collaborations, I had to travel to Europe and meet the expert in magnetism in person. I needed some travel money in advance, given the large budget I had forecasted for the trip. The fact that the locals saw I was not that happy about the work in the lab probably made them even more worried when I requested money in advance to go abroad. The aggravating circumstance that this was happening during the first six months might have precipitated them into believing I wanted to leave the job.

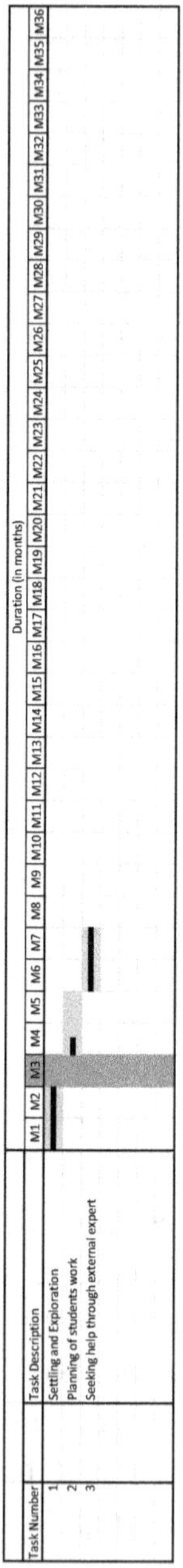

Task Number	Task Description	Duration (in months)																																			
		M1	M2	M3	M4	M5	M6	M7	M8	M9	M10	M11	M12	M13	M14	M15	M16	M17	M18	M19	M20	M21	M22	M23	M24	M25	M26	M27	M28	M29	M30	M31	M32	M33	M34	M35	M36
1	Settling and Exploration																																					
2	Planning of students work																																					
3	Seeking help through external expert																																					

A sort of mental battle ensued, and I felt kind of under siege ever since after that. In my mind, I was behaving very rationally: I could not kick-start some projects I wanted, and therefore I was seeking help from some old colleagues of mine. To me, there was nothing wrong with this. However, the disruption that followed is difficult to put into words. At this point, I realized I had to spend some time away from the workplace. During this precious time-off but at the same time a difficult period for me, I reframed my whole plan. Now that rapport was a bit dented with my superiors, I had no other chance than to follow two separate routes. One route would have been to streamline the lab work when I only worked with those students who seemed keener to learn. I did not discard the rest; I simply dedicated much more attention to the most promising ones. I completely changed the original plan, which now had become Plan A1. This plan was still pretty much down to those few students who wanted to excel. However, now we were after the end of months nine of the project, and I did not have achieved much data collection to produce papers that I originally wanted to. The pressure was mounting by the day. But the extremely high pressure I felt did not crush me. It made my sight much sharper as that of a hawk when hunting.

This was way too risky, and I felt to be on a critical path by the beginning of March (M10). So, I pulled out of my hat Plan B, but did not tell anyone about it. Overall, Plan A1 (which included Plan B) is shown in the following picture. As can be seen, despite I won't tell them, I basically stopped planning for the work of most students assigned to me. I would assist all of them in their pursuits, but their project had basically fallen outside of my project! For those very few good students I selected, I integrated their projects inside my plan and dedicated them to them a lot of time and support. Of these few students, one female student became the best student I ever had. She would seek help, listen to all I had to share, and then very swiftly come up with a plan, implement it, and get to the bottom of the story. She would still need some support during the execution and analysis phases, but I was extremely impressed by how quickly she would grasp ideas and implement them. She was assimilating things like a sponge.

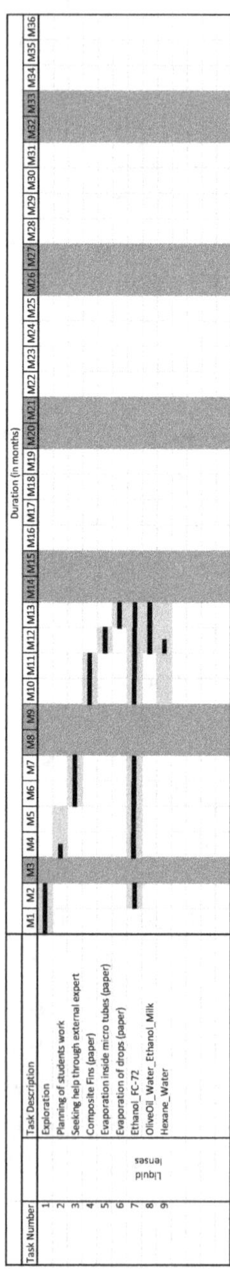

I even beefed up Plan B by pulling an old and unfinished project which I could have concluded in around two months. There were both experimental strands on this Plan B as well as numerical works. I had only four months to pull it up before the summer holidays. I became ruthless with my time. I remember that after setting up an experiment and collecting some useful data on it, I retreated home, and there I spent almost three solid weeks doing some numerical simulations and writing another manuscript. During these three weeks, I basically went out only to fetch food. It was very intense. In the end, all the efforts of these three weeks resulted in one of the manuscripts I feel prouder about for its completeness, its simplicity, and all the sweat that was poured onto it. At the end of April, overall, I had two papers published, one manuscript submitted, and two more in the writing process. A manuscript on liquid lenses was put on the back burner as it required much more analytical treatment. This was a manuscript where I was trying to include some of the tests I did before arriving at this new workplace and some of those gathered here. It has a large number of data to present, but there was some issue with coherence and lack of in-depth analysis, at least according to some reviews I had received on one version of the manuscript I submitted. Here I showed how sometimes it makes sense for the wise hyena to save the stolen prey for a more delicious meal later when other hungry predators are still lingering around.

Between May and the middle of June, I pulled two more manuscripts, albeit the work was not so intense as for the previous paper. Here I used the also some data I had collected before arriving in this new workplace. I submitted these two other manuscripts and then wanted to take a short break before finishing off the manuscript on liquid lenses. During these two months, I also worked most early mornings in the lab doing many tests on other types of liquid lenses, which later would turn to be pivotal for me in learning this new topic from the inside out. And here another disaster struck. I became convinced now that my host institution not only knew about this issue but kept it secret for as long as they could. At this point, I was told to apply to my Embassy for renewing my passport due to expire end of July. With the new passport, I had to apply for a visa again, and my employer had to apply for the work permit. What ensued then was next to ridiculous. However, this affected my working and private lives so much that I lost nearly three months of work. I sensed my host still felt I was unhappy there, and they feared I could leave. Well, by now I was really unhappy. Later on, I realized this would have been a standard fixture: every time I would leave for a while, they would go in fibrillation. And this is how it panned out just before every Christmas and summer holidays.

I was practically forced to go to Europe to renew the passport and applying for a working visa again. And given that I arrived in Europe at the end of June, I could not return to the workplace before they closed for summer vacation. My laptop was left there, and my test results were there too. These three months were frustrating. I could not do any work at all. I was still waiting for the response from journals about my submitted manuscripts as well. Therefore, I tried hard to enjoy this time. I had planned before going back to Europe to go to an Iron Maiden concert in Trieste in July, and this was by far the most enjoyable thing I did that summer. I went alone, and it was even more enjoyable. Then I spent a lot of time at the seaside, went camping, and took my family members to Capri, Sardinia, and for a few days to a spa.

I then returned to my host country at the beginning of September to teach and work in the lab. I wanted to clear all that adrenaline accumulated in my legs because of the last few months of frustration. I planned a 95 km ride by bicycle. This time on my own. I had to stop once at 70 km to get some food as the chocolate bars, and the honey I took with me was not enough. I reached the final destination in 5 hours and 30 minutes (with an almost 30 minutes stop for the light meal). This has been, by far, the most astonishing sport achievement I ever accomplished. And before doing it, I had taken the bike only seven times after a long break from the pedals of nearly four straight months. With this boost of morale, I put my head down and planned some more experiments. I won a small research grant on a magnetic refrigeration concept during the same month of the bike ride; this was one of my boss's topic, and I decided to get involved. Soon after, he took this project away from me and he also messed up with the development of a laboratory wind tunnel to test composite fins for aerospace application at around 100 m/s airspeeds (which is quite a significant value). By now, I understood he was behind all of the significant issues I had in that place. Without him realizing it, I had circled him like a shark circle a prey it cannot see clearly. Having understood the difficult personality he had, I devised a plan to deal with him too. People like him like to destroy what others do. Then I had no other option to take the inhabitants out of some housing compound before inviting him over to destroy the housing. I let him sink two boats (two of the projects I had started) deliberately, as I concentrated on other ideas. These 'boats' he sank were the most visible ones, which maybe he had also problems with his other colleagues, who were seeing the progress I was making. But I went all the way down to almost finishing the wind tunnel to keep him and his difficult close colleagues (among which some students, both male and female) busy thinking I wanted this tunnel at all cost. It was a deliberate sacrificial lamb instead. As another sacrificial lamb was a Stirling Engine's idea, I pulled up almost out of nowhere with an old colleague from the UK. For three years, I witnessed three lamb slain, which I deliberately breed for months.

We are in October of my second year, and I am following Plan A2. One great news arrived at last. The work I did for three solid weeks, almost locked inside the home, paid off. My third paper was accepted. This was a massive boost in morale. From now on I would decide who to work with outside of the university and which project to work on. This outstanding female student I had, finished her master's degree and left the university. I was left with some temporary students who were interested in specific topics and few colleagues who, by now, wanted to learn from some of my legacy projects to see if they could chase some local funding. I tried to help everyone who came to see me. But I stopped going out searching for people to help me in my, by now, rather ramified, always molding, and more intricated project.

At this point, I decided to go for the rest of my project all alone. Everything would have been down to me. Down to how many energies I had to spare. Down to how much time I had left. I could not blame anyone else from now onwards.

With being propped up by the latest paper, I decided to spend the next two months addressing all the shortcomings of the liquid lenses' manuscript. I worked endless hours on this manuscript. I learned so much about surface science, especially that part of this branch of science connected with spreading and floating. End of November, I submitted this other manuscript. I went immediately inside the lab for a few more weeks to finish off some additional tests on different types of lenses and then left for Europe before Christmas. This time there was not much disruption, just some unpaid bills I had to foot carried over in the new year. I was not happy about paying at work for equipment and services with my pocket, but it seems this is the way some countries show how much they love you.

After some nice and at last relaxing holidays with family and friends, I had planned to go to the UK to use an infrared camera. Just before the end of the year, the contact person from which I borrowed the camera a few times in the years before, did not respond to me anymore.

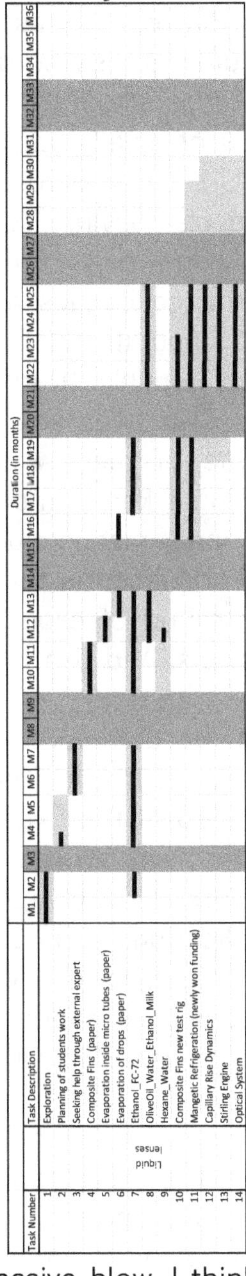

This was another massive blow. I think I know why this happened, but I do not have any proof of it. I had to phone all around Europe to find someone from whom I could rent an infrared camera. I also had to organize for liquid samples to be available in that country as there are regulations about carrying some liquids across borders. I literally spent twenty days searching in the UK, Italy, and Belgium. After tens of calls and hundreds of emails back and forth, I found a rental company in the UK. I managed to find a time slot for the experiments, organize buying liquids, and bring all other samples with me in my bag. From there, I then went to see some new potential colleagues in Germany for a few days and finally to a Computational Fluid Dynamic course of one week in the Czech Republic. During this time, I received two other great news. Two separate journals had accepted two of my papers. One of them was my first paper on liquid lenses. At this point, I knew I needed only one extra article published. I had one manuscript still under review. Upon returning to the workplace, as this was probably not enough, I devised another round of experiments to produce data for two more manuscripts. And this is shown in the picture below with Plan A3.

I produced the data for two more manuscripts, wrote and submitted one of them. Then I was preparing for a conference I attended in the middle of June near Barcelona, and another terrific news arrived. Another paper of mine on a new subject I worked on (evaporation of drops) had been accepted for publication. In just over one year and three months since I decided to pull out of my pocket Plan B, I succeeded in hitting the paper target with five papers in category 1 and one paper in category 2. Actually, I exceed the goal of two journal articles. From there onwards, I still had issues with some of my colleagues, but no longer on matters related to publishing papers.

You might have spotted that even in this articulated and ever-changing plan, I did not use milestones. This is actually true; however, the program's constraints, in essence, were the milestones against which I could measure how well I was doing. The milestones became the end of those strings of four months during my stay at the workplace. Before I left for Europe, I had to have finished all the experiments I wanted and wrote the papers I wanted to write.

Apart from using the infrared camera two times in Europe and going to a training course, I could not do any sizable work away from the workplace.

You notice from Plan A3 that with the last idea on optical system, I even found the time to learn more about an optical system, made a prototype, and tried hard to sell this to a local company. This was not part of my job, but I found extra time and energies for additional activities all along those three years of my stay despite the considerable pressure I had at this workplace.

Now that the story is told and you have seen how many changes (sometimes dramatic, surely drastic, and probably a bit more dreadful that I described in these lines) I had to implement, it is perhaps time to step back from the story understanding the broader context.

When you face a stiff problem or a stubborn person (I actually had both of them in this job), then you must make sure you keep some of your cards hidden. Then you hedge your bets by devising a plan with multiple strands (which means various options for you). You should pour much more effort into those activities which are more down to you; here, you can make a considerable contribution as things are more under your direct control. If I did not have Plan B from the start (when I visited this university the first time and well before I accepted joining it), I would have been much worse off. Instead, having material to build on gave me the reassurance I would have been in a position to hit my target, albeit still facing some stiff difficulties.

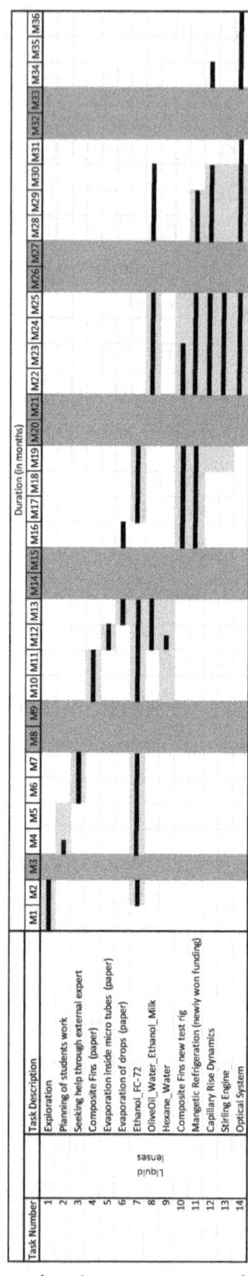

I concentrated on producing papers because I can do the work in the lab, I can post-process the data, and I can write articles myself. I did not concentrate on getting 120,000 Euro funding, despite this might have been seen more doable

(I did get nearly 40,000 Euro at the start of my second year on the magnetic refrigeration proposal). Chasing funding in another country can be tricky for a foreign, as locals are much more connected. I also spread the load on eight projects. Of these, five worked rather well, and three were ditched in the end as 'sacrificial lambs.' Of those five that worked well, three were completely new to me. Therefore, the added benefit is that now I know rather well these new topics, and with the published works on them, I could seek collaborations and even some initial funding in other countries.

As you become more experienced, you will learn how to play your cards well. You will spot well in advance possible issues in the lab and also in relationships. Knowing that you are your own master and that if the difficult person you might face is above you, then this person most likely does not have as much time as you do for your project; therefore, you will always have some advantages over him/her.

When I deal with difficult people at work, I think this way: for them, it is a 'job'; for me, it is 'personal.'

Understanding the balance of power and the dynamics of relationships would give you an ENORMOUS advantage. At times, some learning process can be tough, as it indeed was with me. But when you get to the other side, it would feel empowering.

The last suggestion I like to make is that I do not believe in the say that when something does not work, you 'never give up.' This sounds to me as you face a reinforced concrete wall, and you still keep pushing it. Well, it might never move. What about these two other strategies? You can use a ladder and climb the wall. Or you start removing the soil from its foundation, then using a lever, you might be able to topple it. My last complicated example above shows you from how many directions I tackled the stiff problem I faced. When I made it through, it felt SUPERB in every sense.

The race

3

The donkey's work

A PhD is hard work. At times you will spend long hours solving issues nobody else has ever faced. There is pride in doing this. But there are sacrifices as well. You will notice soon with the next section of this book that I will jump straight into your PhD writing parts. This is done deliberately.

We have equipped you with some key tools and given a rather clear idea of the right mindset a PhD student should have. In Chapter 2 we have seen how to plan for work and some strategies were also given as examples on how to tackle small and big issues.

It is down to you how you will manage the core part of your work. This core part of the PhD is different for each PhD project. This part is by far the longest and it is where you will, hopefully, spent the majority of your energies. It would help if you lay down a work plan that you regularly revise (say every three to six months). The rest is about sailing the sea, avoiding at all costs to sail through storms. And we covered most of this in the previous chapters. There is no need here to repeat that again.

Using the analogy of the Formula 1 race, we will let you run around the circuit for many laps and in this chapter, we will concentrate on one of the most daunting tasks of the race: writing.

Now that this is clear let's dive into your project's writing parts where some general suggestions are of interest to all PhD students.

The writing of your first book and quality thereof

A PhD is like a comet. Make sure you catch it instead of remaining asleep while it ploughs the sky above your head!

Writing a thesis can be a daunting task. It can appear as an insurmountable mountain. It should not be. There is no reason to be. Writing your thesis can, at times, also be fun. As you write it, you will notice how the writing pace changes when you move from things you do not feel enthusiastic about to things that make you tick. Therefore, all you have to do is to write first a thesis outline. Then pivot between the boring parts and those you really want to tell the World about. This approach would make the writing of those less exciting parts of your thesis more bearable.

Defining a suitable thesis outline is the first step towards successfully writing your first book. This is actually what experienced writers do. They do NOT take a blank piece of paper and start writing on it. They have defined a structure for their book before they grab their pen to write and then also scribble on paper.

Look at how many pieces of work you did. If each part of your work is related to a different aspect of your PhD project's broader topic, then maybe this defines the core structure of your thesis. For me, it was really like this. I had tackled my topic from different angles, plus I used three experimental techniques; additionally, in my project's last leg, I also did some numerical work. Therefore, I decided to have the core of my thesis made of four chapters, where the three experimental techniques and then the numerical work were tied to four different aspects of the same topic. After this, I added one chapter as the introduction, which justified why I had been thrilled at doing all those experimental campaigns, followed by a second chapter explaining my chosen topic's broader background. Finally, I added one last chapter summarizing the outcomes of my work.

It felt almost like a patchwork. I developed the core parts and stitched to them the three extra chapters to introduce and close the thesis. What came out was a rather seamless amalgamation of them all. The flow of the script was very fluid. The story I told quite exciting and, at times, intriguing as well. Yet, each chapter had a specific structure itself, and by looking at it from a distance, it seems as each chapter forms a portion of a novel that can be sold separately as epistolary novels do.

Start by making a tentative division of your thesis into chapters. For each chapter, also divide it into sections, and if necessary, sub-sections as well. It is good practice to have a similar layout for each chapter; this will give the right impression of coherence and consistency to the work you have done that you are now presenting to the scientific community.

Remember that your thesis, as well as your papers, will hang out there for a very long time. At least for centuries, if not longer than that. Some students' contribution is so powerful that it becomes a cornerstone in a particular field of knowledge. The work of a few students is so great that they literally transform an industry or solve longstanding scientific problems. With your PhD, you should aim for at least an important to a significant contribution to humankind as well. This is within your reach because you are working on a topic that is already at the forefront of knowledge.

Give a nice flow to the thesis. As in a paper, take the reader through your journey and tell a story. Your PhD's story. In your thesis, you should also include details of those things that you did not finish and those trials that did not work. This is typically left out in scientific papers too, but not only for a matter of limited space. In your thesis, you can also describe step-by-step the different covered aspects, such as: how you set up the experiments; how you constructed the test articles; which is the procedure you devised to run the experiments; and, if there is any particular cleaning procedure that you have developed which pertains to your research topic.

You should demonstrate that you have an excellent understanding of your topic and also know how your specific problem is related to more general ones of much broader scientific interest. This is particularly important when you will try to explain what you have done and why you have done it to others in settings such as conferences or even to friends. For this to sound convincing, you would need to give facts and figures, which are typically found in published works. Thus, you need to keep reading throughout your three years of PhD and include in your thesis a good number of such references. A typical bottom number would be close to a few hundred, at the very least! Something you will be asked repeatedly is how your specific topic relates to applications in the marketplace. It is a good idea to explore this as well if your problem is not already strongly linked to an industrial need/application.

After you write the individual chapters, make sure the way you stack them up flows very well. This is really important to give the reader a sense that you tell an exciting story by making deliberate stops to several scenes where you dive in to enlighten and entertain the reader a bit more. And when a beautiful story is told, it has an opening part in which you make it clear from the outset what an enlightening and exciting journey that one will be. Besides, you somehow need to keep the momentum with the start of each chapter. This is why I have decided to write a short motivation at the beginning of each chapter. You do not have to copy this template. But make sure to put yourself in the reader's shoes and try to visualize how the reader would react when reading your thesis, s/he moves from a chapter to the next. You want the reader to read throughout the entire thesis. This is, by the way, the objective a good book writer strives to achieve. Do not forget the closing of the story. Actually, the end of the story should define how the preceding chapters are lined up to reach a climax and then show how you solved the conflicting needs.

Aim at writing the thesis between three to maximum four months. I have done it in 2,5 months, and I am not a special person; besides, English is not my first language, and back when I started writing papers and then my thesis, I had only practiced English for few years.

A thesis is a written amount of words; better if counted in pages. There is a specific expectation of how many pages a thesis should be. Let's assume that the average is two hundred pages, all-inclusive. Even if you write only two pages per day, that will take you around 3,5 months, which is a reasonable and achievable target. Thus, you should aim at writing at least two pages per day, and you will definitely make it before four months have passed.

Keep a steady pace. You should try and write the same number of pages every day. If that amount is two pages, stick to it, and after a few weeks, it will become a habit. Try to understand when during the day you have the peak of performance. For instance, I am much more efficient in early mornings; therefore, I get to work when there are not many people around yet and get a good chunk of work done. When others populate the office/lab, I enjoy my first short break with them. Taking a day completely off per week is a good plan in any circumstance and workplace. When you switch off completely, your brain processes all that you took in, and you will notice a huge difference when you get back to work on your thesis again.

Write ideas down when you are away from your computer. Our brain is flooded with ideas and thoughts which literally pop up from nowhere. When this happens, try and take a short note of them. These can be truly valuable because, most likely, such thoughts and ideas are really BRILLIANT.

Once you have written a good draft of a section of one chapter, you should let one friend, or better two, read it. They will give you some feedback on your writing style and tell you if they quickly understood the contents. Remember that your thesis is more aimed at the general public than to a specific readership. Papers are targeted to specific readerships; therefore, they are more technical and at times difficult to fully grasp for non-specialists in the area. Your thesis should be written in a way that most people can understand the basics of. This is why for assessing your writing style, you should select a few friends who have no prior knowledge of the topic you have worked on. At this point, make any changes they suggest and then share this section with your supervisor. You should be considerate of your supervisor's other commitments; therefore, avoid dumping on his/her desk/computer screen large chunks of work you did for him/her to review. The supervisor/student relationship is vital for a smoother ride through a possibly tortuous PhD project. With a short section, your supervisor is more likely to read it fast and give you detailed feedback, which will be extremely valuable for you and your morale. You should set some regular sessions with your supervisor, who must read all of your thesis from here onwards. Handle your writings between few days and a week in advance (or longer if your supervisor is very busy during that time) before you sit together to discuss it after s/he has read it.

If you have understood that the reading your supervisor can do amounts to around a chapter per time, then this is ideal. You can probably write a chapter in a couple of weeks and handle it a chapter at a time. This really depends on the two of you and your other commitments. I delivered it in a chapter per time, and it worked absolutely fine.

An important aspect to keep in mind is the quality of the work you do in your PhD. You need to pay proper attention to the contribution you make to the existing body of knowledge. What I mean by this is that planning an experiment, gathering some data, and presenting it does not guarantee that you have made an important contribution to science. As one older friend used to say, a silly but effective example of this is '2 + 2 = 4'; he said to me: 'this is absolutely correct, but it does not give any new or exciting information.'

To really contribute to science, you need to find first and foremost a niche that has not been explored yet. To this end, you would need to critically assess what others before you have done in a specific field of science. Whilst reading other people's work, try and visualize the bounds of the existing research. You are kind of defining the borders of an imaginary country. Within these boundaries, you then have to draw regions that have been more or less covered by other authors. When this exploratory work is mostly done, you can then spot if virgin regions are within the drawn boundaries; these are those areas where you should concentrate. Another more radical possibility is to explore areas outside the boundaries; in this case, if successful, you have an excellent chance to be TRANSFORMATIONAL. In fact, most of the time, science is an evolution process, a rather slow evolution process. Experts keep working on the same subject/s most of their lives. When a revolution is brought in by someone who defies the 'norms', this transformation takes place; sometimes, this transformation leads to the opening of an entirely new branch of science.

With such an approach in mind, you have defined at the very beginning of your project (when your serial experimental work has not really begun yet) the potential quality of your contribution to science. When I started, in the first 6th Months Report of my PhD project, I defined a set of experiments and associated parameters to be monitored for the rest of my PhD project. In this summary, I was pretty much conservative, not having any prior significant research experience in the lab. However, this short document I produced for my 6th Months Report was instrumental in shaping the rest of my project. It turned to be a kind of a compass I used to judge progress. What I did not know at the time I wrote it was that this short document would drive me to produce so many papers in the end, some of which have become a standard in those particular research niches. I did not follow to the letter the content of that 6th Months Report; I actually did much more than was initially envisaged in that document. There were a few items in that document that I never followed up because they became either trivial or remained too challenging to implement. Having said all of this, that short document (which was a requirement by my university at the time) was pivotal in shaping the rest of the work that followed. And this document was almost entirely based on reviewing the literature I could read within the first half a year of my PhD.

I suggest you target to produce some manuscripts after the midterm of your PhD project. To start with, this gives you focus and motivation. Besides, this approach means that you are processing some of the data while you collect it; this strategy is more effective than waiting one year or more to process the data. Papers can go to be part of a chapter or even becoming an entire chapter of your thesis. This means a good portion of your later work in writing your thesis could be done at the time you will write some manuscripts. Therefore, I highly recommend this approach. In case it is not technically possible to write manuscripts, you should aim at writing some technical reports, instead. The time taken for this writing will not be wasted. You will save a lot of precious time later, and it will feel less daunting when you start putting the head down to write the whole thesis during the final year of your PhD.

It is good practice to get your thesis grammatically checked. This is valid for both native and non-native speakers. Your thesis will be held in the university repository, and everybody from around the World can request a copy of your thesis. This does happen quite regularly because a thesis is much more detailed than papers, and usually, a thesis also includes those things that did not work, which you most likely will not want to put down in papers. A thesis also reveals (explicitly or implicitly) the process you went through to narrow down the general topic and how you then selected a niche where you drilled down to carve a place in the scientific community for your work. A thesis also reveals the path you followed to fulfill your original plan and, in case you had to take turns from it, your thesis will reveal why you did so. Finally, a thesis also shows clearly how your selected materials and equipment for your experiments and how you assembled and commissioned these experiments before you performed serial tests on them. This is a precious piece of information for other researchers who, inspired by your work, want to take it further.

Young researchers like you are tempted by the desire to say everything they learned with their writings. I had this temptation too, and it persisted, at times, even after I graduated. Over the years, I noticed that this temptation had basically a strong correlation with me tackling a new subject. It is like I want to 'show the World' that I learned exceptionally well about the new topic I am now writing about. I have resisted this urge over the years, but must admit it is still pretty much there. The suggestion I can give both you and myself here is that we should keep an eye on the length of the writing. A standard paper is between ten and fifteen A4 pages. A Letter has more stringed length requirements (typically four pages or say 2,500 words). A thesis, too, should be limited in length, but it is practically not limited. A thesis of around 200 pages is acceptable. A thesis of 400 pages is way too much. There is also the opposite issue. Some students or even writers struggle in writing down their ideas, and therefore they try to paddle the sides with 'zeros.' This should be avoided at all costs. The reader picks up on these kinds of traits, and the impression s/he will have of your work is of something of diminished quality.

Let me give you one historical example. German aerodynamicist Ludwig Prandtl in 1908 published a cornerstone paper of only sixteen pages. With those sixteen pages, Prandtl changed fluid dynamics forever, as humans knew it. He introduced the boundary layer concept, which is a crucial element in the fluid to solid interaction. Tons of papers and books have since been written on the boundary layer, but none had the profound impact that Prandtl's sixteen pages article made on this branch of science. Not to mention the almost infinitive number of applications that stemmed from boundary layer research since then.

How to turn a rather dull thing into an advantage

Reading references related to a topic you are trying to grasp is like building a PUZZLE. You start building it somewhere, and you have no idea at first how to link these loosely connected, seemingly unrelated parts. The more you read, the more pieces you put down inside the puzzle; the less frightening it looks; the more you start spotting features and start guessing what the final picture might reveal. This is a fascinating and highly rewarding part of doing research, which I am still pretty much in love with these days.

By searching in a physical LIBRARY, you will reach less than an online search on a specific publisher's archives and even less than what you will find by looking at a web-based search engine.

Clearly, reading plenty of references (papers, thesis, books, websites, etc.) can be, at times, boring. If one thinks that throughout a PhD the number of such items can total several hundred, then this becomes a daunting task, indeed. For its nature, being this not our work, it is probably deemed to be felt as an 'imposed constriction.' Is there an alternative path to follow to make the literature review more bearable? The answer is: probably yes. My experience shows that it is: definitely yes!

Let's see how we can achieve even more than just this. Shall we start with a metaphor? Would you get into the driving seat of a Formula 1 racing car without prior training? After all, you might already have by now the driving license, don't you? Thus, why should you worry so much about stepping into that wheeled missile? What are you hesitating about? Just step inside. I have been driving cars for over 25 years. Small cars, big cars. Few times even go-carts. But I would not be that foolish in stepping inside a Formula 1 racing car without some prior training. The speed is so high that even the smallest of lapses might feel like losing a precarious balance on a ledge. It is not exactly the same for a PhD. You will not put your life at risk. However, a PhD is something slightly different from other forms of academic degrees.

It is then wise to invest some quality time in understanding the norm before you stepped up onto the stage. The search itself can be daunting too. However, you might feel much better in knowing that during my undergraduate studies, when I needed a scientific paper, I would go to the engineering library, and if I found the title of the paper I wanted, I would have needed to fill a form. Then the librarian would ask my supervisor for approval, he would pay the small fee, and eventually, around one week after my initial inquiry, I would receive a photocopy of the paper.

Nowadays, with all the software available, you probably do not need to print hard copies of all the papers you read. There is a bit advantage with the soft copies of the references you read. These files can migrate with you once you finish your PhD, which is harder to do with heavy paper copies.

I will not suggest which search engines you can use to check for scientific papers and specific book. All publishers have dedicated search engines you can use even from home for free, to read at least the abstract. There is an effort done by publishers and authors alike to publish papers as Open Access. This means that the authors foot the total cost to publish their work, and their work is freely accessible forever to all people of the World who simply have an internet connection and a device to connect to it. Google Scholar is a free to use platform under Google, where you can also search for papers, books, patents. It gives you information about the citations a paper has attracted and you can explore if the author/s have a Google Scholar account as well, which provides you with value-added information. All you need, in this case, is a Google account.

It is a good idea to use a free patent search also to scan for potential filed and granted patents on your subject.

Patents give a completely different perspective than paper. They are more biased towards design, and maybe you can get inspired about components of the test rig you will later design and build.

Whatever you read, my suggestion to you is to highlight the relevant parts of the references you learn and summarize it. My experience teaches me that between five and ten lines are usually enough for those more general papers on your subject. In case you find an article that is really close to your topic, you probably wish to report more about it in your future thesis. This sort of summary seems a burden at this point in time as you are years before you will write the thesis. But actually, this approach is almost your 'savior' when it comes to write your thesis. At that point, you might well have forgotten the contents of the references you read. Almost inevitably, you will also forget where you read something you vaguely remember. For these reasons, it is good practice to summarize each useful reference you learn that you want to cite in your thesis.

Do not forget that you will also write some papers. And some of these references might well be going down in your articles as well. You won't believe, but following this approach, my whole thesis was written in 2,5 months (from 8:30 am to 5 pm and only during weekdays), while I would still play football with my peers, run around the city every couple of days, and going out with my girlfriend. The literature review was, for me, one of the easiest parts to integrate into my thesis. I had written most of it already during the previous years. It was just a bit more articulated than the act of copying-and-pasting from my notes.

One crucial aspect is how to name and store the electronic copies of the references you read. My suggested approach is to separate the references into folders that match the chapter name you will write in the thesis. This choice of mine was driven by the decision to include references at the end of each single chapter of my thesis. Inside each folder, I prefer to name a paper with the name of the authors, the acronym for the journal, and the publication year. Something such as the following examples from my current work:

Fernandez-Homsy_JFM-2003

Saylor_et-al_PoF-2000

Of course, you can choose any way you wish to store your files. Just make sure you use an approach that is as mnemonic and as consistent as possible. I tend to remember more researchers' names and then journal names. I am rather bad at remembering the paper title and the publication year.

The literature review is a process. It starts right after you begin your PhD project, and it ends while you are writing the thesis. Actually, it can go beyond this point. In fact, you might be writing papers after you submit your dissertation and therefore, you might well add a few more references to your already long list. Doing the literature review is like climbing a pyramid. The higher you get, the narrower it becomes. However, the more specialized it becomes, the broader your view will be. And this is exactly what you will feel as you gain experience and acquire new knowledge. In the process, the literature review will make you feel that you are really holding your subject at your fingertips.

How many references should you read? Well, this is a similar query to 'how long is a piece of string?' I think it really depends on how rich and old the subject you have chosen to tackle is; it also depends on how much attention your subject has received over the years. Remember that you do NOT necessarily need to read everything on your subject during the span of your PhD. You would surely want to read the critical works published on the same problem you are tackling. In my case, I cited exactly 222 papers in my thesis (including 41 articles cited in the two appendices), and I read in total over 1,200 items between papers, thesis, books, and specialist websites.

It is absolutely great to feel empowered, experienced, and knowledgeable. However, there is a potential pitfall with this. One might get complacent in thinking s/he knows everything after a few months and does not feel anymore the need to learn more. But do not get too much surprised. Some professors do the same when they embrace a new subject. And at times, some professors develop a rather narrow view because of biases they might have. So, my suggestion here is to stay hungry for learning more. The same happens in every sector of society. How do you avoid this pitfall? Only by hinging on your humility, by realizing you have two ears and one mouth for a specific reason, and by making sure you keep at least one eye open on technology development in your field as time passes on in your PhD.

Now comes probably the most crucial suggestion I want to make. A literature review is NOT merely citing someone else work. To be powerful and to make your contribution to knowledge stand out, you might want to consider being critical about the references you read and cite. Mention the shortcoming of these references and point out what instead you will do or would have done to address some or all these shortfalls. This way, you show the reader you have greatly benefitted from assimilating the teaching of the references you read. Your literature review is NOT merely parroting what the reader of your thesis/paper can find elsewhere. And with time, you will become more and more critical when you read other people's work. A point will come when from the very beginning of the paper you are reading, you will start standing out of the paper; kind of hovering on top of the words you are reading, which allows you to have a more holistic view of what the authors are taking you through the lines of their work. As you become more critical, you will also start spotting mistakes and especially understand if the authors have deliberately hidden something. Unfortunately, some unscrupulous authors fabricate their results or twist their experimental technique for presenting results that could not possibly be obtained with that particular technique or procedure. This sort of tactic undermines the noble idea behind publishing scientific work. And you can easily understand how there could be a snowball effect once a faked paper is published and becomes a standard in the industry, without no one spotting as questionable. Other researchers that follow tend to 'conform' to the norm. Therefore, there is a real possibility that artificially created trends (or at the very least 'forced trends') get established in the scientific community. By becoming an expert in critically reading a paper, you might not only stop this but even reverse the trend; and you might gain vast popularity for having done so. As time progresses, you might even be invited to be a reviewer of manuscripts submitted to journals for publication. This might start from your supervisor passing you a manuscript to review for him/her. If I were you, I would take such a task on with enormous pleasure. It is an excellent training ground, and you start contributing to the scientific community differently as well.

Attending conferences

The idea of traveling abroad to attend a conference is really a tempting one for a PhD student. Probably for two main reasons. Firstly, there is the thrill of traveling, which in many cases means also traveling overseas. This in itself is a massive magnet most ordinary people would find it difficult to resist. In the case of a young PhD student, this opportunity also means a short 'holiday' on the side of the important event the student will attend. Typically, the conference organizers are really attentive in picking a site and a particularly attractive venue for all conference attendees. The program's schedule is made in a way that there is a perfect mix of activities: formal activities like presentation slots, poster sections, and plenary talks are staggered between more ludic activities such as organized tours to specific attractions, lab tours, special conference dinners. Not to mention the more than generous offers of meals and numerous coffee breaks during which students have an almost unique opportunity to meet leading scientists around the World. These scientists do not only attend the conference to present their work, but many of them also attend to meet colleagues and young folks like you. After all, many of them understand all too well that some of you will be coming up to replace them as they retire from active academic posts. Attending students will also measure themselves against their peers, bringing so many different viewpoints and coming from so many diverse corners of the World.

The second big thrill for a PhD student attending a conference is the idea to present his/her work to an expert audience. It is both the size of the audience, the location away from the office/lab, and the added difficulty that most of the scientists at the conference are new to you. How to reframe this rather 'scary picture?' What about this line of thought? You are a young researcher, and like you, all other young folks are there for the first time to learn from more experienced scientists. Admittedly, these experts know that very well; they have been in your shoes many years before. They want you to feel welcome and valued, or at the very least, listened to. They have a vested interest in you returning to this event again in the future. In fact, most conferences are part of a series of events held annually, bi-annually, or sometimes even every four years, the very existence of which is based on regular and devoted attendees. For this very reason, you should feel relaxed. You will see several scientists approaching you at the conference, especially if you have a poster to display. Stay near the poster, and many people will not only pass by, but they will ask genuine questions and might even be interested in knowing more about the work you are presenting. At those few events I also go, I do the same; I go around and try my best to learn from what I see and even get sometimes inspired about the work other people present. At many conferences I have been in the past years, I have also seen very senior scientists walking along the poster sections and ask specific queries to young people like you. In some cases, the senior scientists have been given the task to rank the posters and at the end of each poster section, the top posters are awarded a gift each.

One word of caution is the following. Do not abuse of attending conferences. It is best to attend conferences during the last year of your PhD, for two reasons. Firstly, because by then, you will have a large body of data to show. You might be writing a journal article, and therefore attending a conference is an excellent opportunity to 'taste the water' with the manuscript you are preparing. You might have valuable feedback from the conference attendees, which can lead to critical improvements in the contents of the manuscript you are preparing. The second vital aspect is that, being at the last leg of your project, you might be thinking already of where to go next in your career. A conference is usually attended by academic institutions, public and private research centers, and companies as well. There is a great chance you might even find plenty of job opportunities there. Keep an eye on the posters and listen to announcements at the conference venue. People advertising available posts in their university are very visible and loud about it. This is what I have seen more and more in recent years.

During the conference, you should also actively approach young folks like you. Spend time together and network with them. They might know someone who knows someone else who is looking to hire you! In May 2004, on the way to a national conference in Warwick, I stopped by Newcastle Upon Tyne and, meeting at a pub a guy who had previous connections with my supervisor, I found my first job in industry. Of course, I went to a formal interview after that, but this person was leaving that company for personal reasons, and he presented my name to his managerial team. I was basically given an important 'business card' by that guy who I had met only twice before for a small project.

To conclude this section, there are two last things I wish to add. One of these is that in general and also for very experienced scientists, attending one very good conference per year, where you present a paper, is more than enough. Why do I say this? It takes me around a few weeks to prepare an eye-catching presentation from carefully selected material for a conference and prepare an inspirational speech. Then there is the travelling to and from the conference which can consume between three to four days up to one week, depending on how large and how far the conference is. It does not end here. During the meeting, I make contacts, and then, upon my return to my office, I think about which contacts to approach for potential collaboration. In case I then go to visit their labs or organize their visit to my lab, this whole post-conference process can consume up to one extra month. These days, many conferences try to publish the best papers into a special issue of a journal they are affiliated with. If this happens, you have a preferential route to get your first paper published in a short period of time. This can still consume a few weeks of your valuable time in editing your original conference paper. You see! It is a rather time-consuming exercise. You probably want to consider squeezing everything possible out of a conference you attend to get a huge 'bang for your bucks,' basically.

The other aspect is about deciding which conference to attend. Choosing a conference is important as the added benefits can be substantial. Therefore, do not be only attracted by how exotic the conference location is and how shiny the venue looks. Read the details carefully the conference organizers have published on the conference website. Since my PhD time (2001-2004) there are plenty of sites grouping upcoming conferences in specific fields. You should check this regularly as from the time the organizers close the submission of papers to the actual meeting, there could be a few good months. Check also who are the key scientists attending the conference to see if anyone is working in the same area as you; this might be a unique opportunity to meet them in person. If this is your added aim, then maybe you wish to consider the chance to get in touch with them, say, between one and two months before introducing yourself, your work, and finding a good technical reason why you want to talk to them at the conference. Check the plenary speakers too and what they will present; typically, the topic they will talk about is defined very early on during the conference's organization.

If I were you, I would select some possible conferences to go to and share this shortlist with the supervisor/s. The supervisor has plenty of experience and can recognize at a glance which conference is worthwhile going to and those who are a simple 'show off by a circle of friends.'

Good luck! And make the most of it.

How to write an enlightening scientific paper

Writing a paper could actually be a palpable scary task. As a matter of fact, it is!

But probably not for the reasons you, at first, might think. In reality, writing a paper can be hugely rewarding and even fun at times.

I have written a number of papers. Some were just 'papers.' Some others were 'quite something.' In many other cases, I felt I was literally 'carving in with my pen' into either a virgin slab of wood or, even better, on an aging piece of wood sculpture where I was determined to leave my print. And so, I did!

We might be fooled by the conventional wisdom that only students of the best universities in the World can write superb papers. Or that our supervisor is an established luminary in the field. Or even that the project we work on is trendy. Well, this is, in part, true. But it is not always the case. You can be working at a good university, have a supervisor who is relatively new to research, and even work on a subject that is only marginally trendy. And yet, you can produce such pieces of handcrafted work that it becomes a standard in that field.

Do you think this is not possible? Do you think this is very far away from you? Do you think you will not be able to match or even surpass this? Think again! Right now, you are grabbing words from a mind that did some of that. And this mind is determined to guide you through, firstly, in seeing things in the same light as it sees them. Then motivate you in striving to achieve more, using fewer energies, and in less time. And finally sharing with you a structure that will allow you to write rather captivating pieces of scientific work. The structure is the most important thing when someone takes a pen with the intent to leave anything printed on paper.

What we are going to do now is to define a basic structure of a manuscript aimed at showing you how the authors get the best of their work by using structure and language to engage the readership.

Shall we begin?

A great scientific paper starts with planning the experiment. Science is not like fiction. You can have a unique style of writing that would make most people drop their jaws, but this is not what a reader of scientific work searches for in a paper. Science follows a sequence of steps, the current form of which was developed for the first time by Galileo Galilei at the beginning of the 17th Century.

A superb paper starts with curiosity. The curious and inquisitive mind of a child is the right attitude to do research. You will try several combinations of parameters in the lab until you find the right mix, which is most likely to give you a 'big bang for your bucks.' Here, with 'bucks', we mean your time and energies.

In my best papers (from the first few ones I published), I have pictured in my mind how good they would have been from the first time I saw something peculiar through a microscope eyepiece. It was just a clue what I had. I had to prove it in many different settings. I showed it to other people familiar with my subject (notably my two supervisors). Then I repeated it again and again on different days and at different times of the day. When I became convinced this was a real phenomenon, I set on a 'hunting mission.' During this part of the project, I allow myself little distractions. I was really ruthless with time. For a few days or few weeks (depending on how complex the task was) I feel like I dive deep inside the ocean. How deep I usually go is down to me. I am in full control during this phase. When I am satisfied, I start resurfacing with my precious catch in my hands.

This is the time to give me a small but precious reward. I usually take one full day off and do something completely unrelated to work. I might invite a friend for a nice meal as well, and typically I do not talk about specific things related to my project. The following day is when I start going through cycles of careful observation of the data I have gathered in the lab. It is not uncommon that I have to return to the lab for repeating few tests run or do some brand-new ones I did not plan, but now I see the need for from the observation of the data already collected.

The following step is to extract the most impressive set of data and produce graphs, plots, and tables. The data I will present in the paper is aligned with my original goal: what I want to show with the paper. This is extremely important because usually, you will collect much more data than the one needed for the article you have in mind to write. And you really do not want to throw inside your paper too many ideas together. Too many opinions will mean a somewhat blurred focus, and this might result in a reduced impact on the readership. I have made this mistake a couple of times. Too many results probably loosely connected end up in a rather long and articulated paper. The paper can be long, but best if it has only a few coherent ideas thrown in, which you will fully develop.

Writing a paper is a craft. My motto is: 'A voracious reader makes a prolific writer.' This is true not only of how much you learn to write but also about the structure and the spin you learn others give to their written work. This is extremely important as it allows you to literally take the reader of your paper through an exciting or even fascinating 'journey.' And your grand goal should be that you inspire some of your readers so much that they will take your subject and develop it further. This means that they will cite your work, and you can continue 'selling your crafted paper' for years, if not decade, or even probably centuries to come.

It is a good idea to start drafting the paper from the Introduction. Here you should take the reader through a 'funnel.' You will start with one or two general sentences that capture the broader subject. Soon after, you begin citing relevant published work following wherever possible a timeline. One of the typical mistakes in this section is to stuff in many loosely related references. This is a terrible practice. I always read the Introduction section of every paper I am interested in. The Introduction is a kind of a 'stage' on which scientists elevate their work onto. You want to do an excellent job at this elevation. As you cite other references, you should be critical of them. Just saying what they have done is not sufficient. You might want to consider saying what they have not done. Or even question what they have done and the conclusions they reached. This approach naturally helps you elevating your work on that stage we mentioned before. By being critical about the already published work, you will also fully justify why you felt a need to launch your project.

After taking, step by step, your reader through a 'funnel' that points him/her to your elevated stage, then it is good practice to finish the Introduction section with a short paragraph mentioning what you will present in the paper. This way, you are setting some expectations in the reader's mind, and it is more likely that the reader will be excited to explore the subsequent sections of your paper.

At this point comes a section you should know inside out. For experimental work, it is the description of the setup and how you operated the rig. For numerical work, this is the section where the code is described with enough details. How many details should you give? Again, that seems similar to the question: 'how long is a piece of string?' Typically, it is good practice to think this way: give enough details that a reader skilled in the art can reproduce it. What does this mean? Well, if your work is about a magnetic refrigeration machine, then a scientist in civil engineering is not supposed to grasp it after the first read. But anyone connected with refrigeration should be able to understand in full what you have done. Practically, this means that you should mention things such as the test rig components and how they work together; but not digressing in describing how a thermocouple or a cartridge heater or even a pressure sensor works.

You should still mention all components used (including thermocouples, pressure sensors, flowmeters, etc.), their characteristics, and the manufacturer. If it is critical to the rig's operation, you should also tell how the apparatus has been assembled and then put into action.

Then comes the critical but often forgotten error analysis. Even a numerical code has errors and they should be stated. There are two kinds of information that you should give. First of all, you should show that you have repeated the experiment several times while you measured the same critical parameters; from these measurements, then you estimate the error at posteriori. Typically, I repeat the test five times and then use some simple statistics such as average and standard deviation to represent the range of errors I make and show how good my results are. Now you are aware that if you have different input parameters feeding in the output parameter you want to present results about, then there are well-known methods to extract the combined output error from the errors of individual input parameters (Kline and McClintock, 1953; Moffat 1988). The other aspect you should consider mentioning is the sensitivity of your instruments. Most processes are time-dependent, and if the devices are slower than the process you want to measure a parameter of, then the data you are going to present is not good enough. Sensitivity gives an idea of how quickly the instrument you are using responds to changes in the measured parameter. In contrast, error analysis provides the precision and accuracy of a measurement. Precision tells you how repeatable your measurement is; accuracy estimates how close a measurement is to the 'expected true value.' Note that, in general, the actual value of anything you want to measure is NOT known.

After describing the experimental setup and procedure, it is time to get your hands itchy. The part that follows is the real contribution to the knowledge you make. This is not a small thing. This is the core of your work, which goes beyond your actual paper. You will spend considerable time collecting the raw data, some other valuable time in postprocessing it, and additional precious time producing suitable graphs illustrating what you intend to show the World. You should describe clearly and concisely each figure, plot, and table you embed in the text of your manuscript. If read on its own, the text should be enough for the reader to understand the main features of the data you are reporting. You can decide if to elaborate further on each set of data you present or dedicate a following separate section. Whatever your choice, critically discussing the results you present is a significant part of your paper. In the majority of cases, just showing the data is NOT enough to get your article published.

Make sure the set of data presented and the arguments brought to interpret them are coherent and organized in a way that flows well. At this point, the sensible idea is to show what you wrote so far to a few people. Let them read your text with the figures and ask them if they grabbed what you tried to portray. Ask them precisely how easy it was for them to read the book and follow your argumentations explaining the set of data plotted in the figures.

Then come the Conclusions section. Here you will summarize with text the main points elaborated in the paper. You do not usually have a word limit for the Conclusions, but some journals that publish Letters do not have this section at all (because of the strict word count limit).

Do not forget the Acknowledgment section. Here you mention the key people, not in the authors' list, who have made a SIGNIFICANT contribution to the work. They can be a professor in a different group, school, or university who has critically reviewed your paper, making essential suggestions for changes; they can also be some technicians who have built a critical component for your tests. But you should not thank your colleagues, friends, partner, and family members just because they exist! This can be done in your thesis, instead. Mention also the funding body and the grant number of your project. They deserve recognition for the lifeblood they provided you with.

The number of cited works you put down in the References is variable. Only some journals would impose a maximum number of references. My suggestion is that you mention those references very relevant to your work. There is no need to cite fifty references in your paper. Your paper is NOT a review paper on the subject; it is a contribution to the topic. I would say that thirty references are already too many and ten probably too few. Between fifteen and twenty-five references is perhaps a good bet. Keep an eye on self-citation. You might not have published papers of your own yet, but your supervisor could have some. In case you cite them, make sure you do not steal the stage. For instance, if you cite twenty papers in your manuscript, then citing between two and three of your own is more than enough. More and more journals ask their reviewers to check on this as part of the reviewing process.

Now comes the Abstract. You see! We did not talk about the Abstract until this point. Why? Because the Abstract does not only condense the ideas you brought to light to solve a particular problem. It also shows, at a glance, the primary outcomes of your investigation. To have a clear idea of which results are most impressive and worth including in the Abstract, you need to wait until all data has been presented and discussed in the paper. The Abstract is what people read after having found your paper on online search engines. They read the Title and the authors, and soon after, they dive inside the Abstract. For this very reason, you MUST make sure the Abstract flows as smooth as a river of oil. The Abstract should be short and a kind of 'descriptive' account of your work. As a descriptive piece of writing, your Abstract should be a bit attractive. Remember, you will either make the reader feel the urge to continue reading your paper or make the reader turn his/her sight away. If possible and relevant, use some more captivating words such as: 'substantially improved'; 'significant increased'; 'paradigm shift'; 'a breakthrough'; 'a discovery'. Do not overstate it. For instance, finding a technical solution with the shape and sizing of a heat exchanger could warrant the use of 'substantially improved' but not that of 'a discovery.'

Finally, it is time to think carefully about a Title for your work. This is even harder than the Abstract. For some journals, the limit here is counted in characters and not words! With the Title, you want to capture the subject and portray your study's most important finding. A couple of examples of titles from real published papers are reported below:

'Edge states on graphene ribbon in magnetic field: interplay between Dirac and ferromagnetic-like gaps'

'A novel approach for heat transfer enhancement in composite fins'

'Breathing, crawling, budding, and splitting of a liquid droplet under laser heating'

As you can see, the first example shows a Title less attractive than the second, despite it is much more inclusive. And the third example is much more intriguing than the second. In the second example, 'novel approach' and 'enhancement' are words specifically introduced to increase the expectations of the reader. In the third example, the 'Breathing, crawling, budding, and splitting' sequence is almost taking the reader through what the liquid droplets have actually experienced in the tests. This description is almost a personification of the experiment.

Learning how to learn

In this session, I am going to show you my style of writing on a scientific topic. This is an adaptation of one of my research fields to a general topic that almost everybody can grasp.

We will start by asking ourselves how some very tall trees (more than 60 m) can bring water and nutrients up to their leaves. It starts with this fact being an attentive observation. This topic is still a controversial matter where there is NOT a universal theory that explains everything, rather some plausible conjectures that give some hints of where to further look at for a better understanding of this ancient and yet quite intriguing subject these days.

I have chosen to write something from scratch instead of taking a well-cited published paper or even one of my own best articles because I want to guide you through the thought process and especially the planning that precedes the generation of a rather intriguing investigation. As you will learn throughout this exercise, most of the time, you do NOT need to have huge budgets and superb laboratory equipment to produce some quite inspiring work. Many times, behind your success is a simple yet powerful single idea that you might have been inspired by reading some piece of reporting/news that has literally captivated you, to the extent that you set on a mission to unveil what others could not quite do yet.

You have probably already spotted how ideas are generated. Your brain is like a pot full of water placed on the hob. When its temperature goes up, at a specific point, ideas popup like the bubbles generating and rising from the bottom of the heated pot. This is actually by far the most VALUABLE part of your work. Idea generation is the basis of groundbreaking work. And you might be amazed at the fact that all human beings are a heated pot of bubbling water most of the time. Unfortunately, for most of us, the water that fills this incredibly imaginative pot is actually poisoned; we tend to be attracted toward negativity and cannot stir the water in the pot in a way that exploits all of those stunning ideas we have every single day. In the majority of cases, we seem to have an incredible and almost uncanny capability to thwart the thoughts that would have led to great ideas and intuitions. Instead, we have 'learned' how to get attached and being span by those thoughts that destroy our imagination, consume a lot of our energies, and subtract a lot of our precious and limited time. Over the years, I have learned how to unravel from this trail of self-destruction. In the process, my imagination skyrocketed, I become the master of my life, and although I am involved in serval projects or doing lots of things in a day, I still have the feeling that a lot of time is left for other more ludic activities.

Now let's return back to the generation of powerful ideas. You do not get up one morning and tell yourself: 'today I am gonna make a discovery or I am gonna invent something.' Instead, you know quite well the subject already and get inspired by something or someone that could well be not very much aligned with your research. However, their contribution is key to that leap forward you are going through now. This is what basically intelligence is: the ability to transpose what you learn in one subject to a different one. To do this, you want to keep READING, and to READ about science, and READING about almost everything else. Reading is like the water level in the pot described above. The more water is there, the larger number of bubbles can be generated or the bigger the bubbles can become.

Coming back to this section's original focus, how did I link one of my research topics with trees? This is the puzzle now. Well, one of the topics I have been working on for a long time is connected with surface tension. However, I had been looking at a transparent capillary tube, which I partially filled with alcohol. I never bothered about the process of filling the tube; I was rather interested in the convective pattern that forms when one of the liquid menisci was positioned near one of the mouths of the tube. Mine is a typical controlled experiment in the lab.

One day in 2018, a younger and ambitious colleague of mine wanted to learn about this topic I had been working on for so many years. After I gave him some references to read and my PhD thesis, he got so excited that he asked me if we could work together on this topic in the lab. I had already started new programs and did not have much time for this. But I did not want to crash his enthusiasm. So, I told him that he seemed so keen that I could not just let him repeat what I did already on the subject. I needed some time to read and then think about a different variation of the same basic experiment I had studied and characterized for years.

While reading some references for inspiration, I came across a paper that mentioned the capillary rise of water in trees. Surely, I had known by then that trees get water and nutrients up their leaves by using some sort of natural pumping mechanism. If you ask most people familiar with capillarity, they would also suggest that this is the way water flows up trees. This of the water flowing inside trees is a natural experiment, one which is not controlled as my experiment in the lab is, instead. So, I was not discovering 'hot water' here. But something new inspired my imagination. A kind of bubble popped up in my brain. I asked myself: how can a liquid like water rise for tens of meters if my alcohols inside capillary tubes rise only of few centimeters? I immediately set off on a quest to find out. I took a pencil, paper, and a calculator and did some rough calculations. I used the following general formula for the capillary rise to determine the maximum rise of a column of liquid inside a pore. But I used the formula in the reverse order. I wanted to find the smallest pore size that would allow water to rise 60 m, as for a tree in a tropical rainforest. This led to:

$$h = \frac{2\,\gamma}{\rho\,g\,r}; \qquad\qquad r = \frac{2\,\gamma}{\rho\,g\,h} = \frac{2\;\;0.0708}{1{,}000\;\;9.8\;\;60} = 2.4\;10^{-7}m = 0.24\;\mu m\;!$$

The aforementioned is the simplified Jurin's law derived in 1718, where h is the capillary rise of the liquid column, γ is the liquid surface tension, ρ is the liquid density, g is the gravitational acceleration, and r is the pore radius.

While a pore of 0.24 mm inside wood certainly exists, the problem is that I used as the surface tension that of pure water (de-ionized, which has literally nothing dissolved in). When particles or other liquid components are dissolved inside water, its surface tension is usually dramatically reduced. Another important factor is the contact angle (which I have deliberately omitted in the generalized Jurin's law reported above), which sometimes reduces by a factor of 2 or even more the capillary rise. At this point, something did not look right. I went back reading more about how water moves in trees.

The references I went reading to learn about the topic revealed that it is highly disputed what produces the rise of water and nutrients inside trees from the roots up to the leaves, which at times can reach 60 m above the ground level. Whatever the dominant mechanism is, one thing had become clear by now. This is still a highly publishable area. The fact that the scientific community does not understand the mechanism very well is an excellent indication that there is scope for you to leave a print on this topic. And this became my quest. Over the course of one year and NOT being this the main focus of my research, I conducted several preliminary tests on capillary rise dynamics. I split the original topic into three sub-topics. One of these three strands I left it with my colleague. The other two, I have been tackling them separately.

What started as a helping hand offered to my colleague, has inspired me so much that I dedicated some considerable time to it afterward.

At this point, it is time that I show you how I would write a short article from some visual observations and measurements I made on corner fingers inside capillary tubes with square cross-sections. It is one of the three strands of capillary rise dynamics I generated from the observation of water rising inside tall trees. This is NOT an actual manuscript. It is a stripped-down version of it; however, it shows you clearly and concisely how to frame your paper to interest the reader and, of course, before the reader, to impress also the reviewers. Remember that reviewers are the gatekeepers of scientific publications. They pretty much decide what gets published and what does not.

I start writing the manuscript ONLY AFTER I have got a powerful idea, I have done the experiments, and I have seen that these experiments might contain something exciting. What is interesting? For me, interesting is something peculiar, non-conventional, or even better if it defies the norm. In this latter case, you can be assured your future paper will significantly impact the scientific community. And this is what you are there for. If you achieve this, you will influence the scientific community on that topic over time, and you will also gain respect from the same community.

The section I write first of the manuscript is the INTRODUCTION. Here I take the reader through a funnel. Start with a couple of broad statements about the broader subject, and then as the words unravel in front of the reader's eyes, his/her horizon gets squeezed through an increasingly narrow passage. It is a passage I deliberately create to take the reader on the contribution I made to this subject. In the following, I will propose a few paragraphs that do just that. The length of these paragraphs and the number of cited references should be deemed right for your manuscript as well. I am simply showing you a method I use to help minimize the words I spent describing what can be already found elsewhere; and make my work stand out, which is instead unique as cannot be found elsewhere.

"Capillary rise is a rather old subject which has attracted notable scientists over the past three centuries. Despite its conceptual simplicity, capillary rise remains to these days only a partially solved problem when applied to real cases. In 1718 the English physiologist Jurin was the first to correlate the rising height of a liquid column with the liquid properties and the pore size. In particular, Jurin's law states that the capillary height is directly proportional to the liquid surface tension (that pulls the liquid up the pore wall) and inversely proportional to both the liquid density and the pore radius. Jurin's law says that the rise increased significantly for the same liquid, reducing the pore size.

Since the pioneering work of Concus and Finn (1969), a significant amount of research has been done on the capillary rise in non-circular cross-section pores. This is because the rise of liquid inside the corners forms a kind of fractal arrangement with the rise of the main meniscus below the fingers in the corners. The liquid rise dynamics in the corners is practically the same as that of the main meniscus. However, Concus and Finn (1969) show that there are limitations on the angle of the corner with the contact angle of the liquid ($<$ pi/2). The other significant contribution of the corners is that the actual radius of the corners is much smaller than the radius of the main pore and this means that the liquid rises much higher in the corners. This results in a significant capillary rise when corners are present in a non-circular tube with respect to circular cross-sections with no corners.

One of the most natural capillary rise applications is the flow of water and nutrients inside a tree, which are moved from the roots up to the leaves from where water evaporates into the surrounding air. Sometimes, in places like tropical rainforests or pine trees or the large redwood forests (https://www.scientificamerican.com/article/how-do-large-trees-such-a/), some trees reach significant heights. This usually is due to their quest to reach sunlight. There is still controversy as to what is the primary mechanism by which water and nutrients reach such heights. Capillary force action is certainly a candidate. However, some scientists have postulated that osmosis might be more critical than capillarity inside very tall trees. It could also be that a combination of the two mechanisms is at play.

While still many aspects related to the fascinating action of capillarity have to be solved, the capillary rise law clearly demonstrates that the size and the shape of the pore are vital parameters, regardless of the pulling mechanism that actually takes place. And in the present work, we will pay close attention to what contribution do corners make to the evaporation from a square cross-section tube and compare it with a circular tube."

What I did in the previous INTRODUCTION is first to introduce (1st and 2nd paragraphs) the subject giving some historical developments. Soon after, I gave further insight into the significant contribution of the cross-section corners (3rd paragraph). In the 4th paragraph, I mention an application of capillary rise found in Nature, which shows some controversy (controversy is a perfect to have in the published literature in order to maximize the chance of producing a significant contribution to knowledge with your work). We moved from capillary rise at the beginning of the passage to evaporation at the end of it, as if evaporation is the focus of our proposed research. In fact, this is the actual focus. Water keeps moving up the trees because there is evaporation from the leaves, which pulls other water up. It boils down to the shape of the meniscus formed at the leaves between liquid and air. This shape determines the pressure drop across the curved interface and, therefore, the level of pumping due to capillary forces that can be produced.

EXPERIMENTAL SETUP AND PROCEDURE

The next part is your bread and butter. I do not think it makes much sense to give you a sort of template for this part. Instead, I give you some suggestions based on my own experience as an author and especially as a reviewer. You should describe your experimental apparatus (or numerical method if your PhD is about numerical work) in detail. All I can suggest here is to be precise and concise. This is NOT a chapter of your thesis. You should write enough for the reader to be able to understand what you have done and how you have done it for the reader to be able to repeat the experiment, if the reader wants. Do not forget things such as the sensitivity of your instruments and your measurements' accuracy and precision. If possible, show this also in the plotted data with error bars, so readers can visually grasp how reliable your measurements are. If your experimental setup is simple, an actual photograph is usually enough. However, if the setup is really complicated or rather large in size, then a scheme is more appropriate; maybe on the scheme, you can put small photographs next to the main components shown on the scheme.

RESULTS

The section in which you describe your experimental/numerical results is the most innovative contribution you make with your manuscript. While following some sort of template, this part is unique in the sense that you are supposed to be the only author presenting this data for the first time. Make the most of it by impressing while keeping it readable and use language to keep the reader interested.

I do not have a fixed scheme for this part. Sometimes I tend to split this part into sub-sections. In the first sub-section, I might simply report the results. In a subsequent sub-section, I fully explain them. In a few cases, I also used a third sub-section to develop a simplified analytical model that I then compare with the experimental evidence. It is down to your preferences and to how many results you want to present. The more you have, the better it is to divide this section into sub-sections.

A general suggestion is that you do NOT need to drop into your manuscript all the results you have. Otherwise, in the end, it will look more like a technical report than a paper. Just select the most relevant results you have. Pick those results which are more eye-catching and show unexpected trends. These are those who will deliver you a huge 'bang for your bucks.' Stay also careful at not presenting the same data more than once. This sometimes happens when plots, graphs, and tables containing similar data are used simultaneously. Also, consider that you can say in words what you see in a graph similar to a previous one you have already thoroughly described. For instance, you have parameter A, parameter B, and parameter C playing a role in an experiment. You show a temperature plot of your test article with changing parameter A. You fully explain what you see. Then you do the same for parameter B. Let's assume for a moment that the change in temperature of your test article with parameter A is represented by an increasing trend going up 12% from its starting value. For parameter B the same growing trend leads to 26% increase in temperature. In case that the change of temperature with parameter C still follows an upward trend, say, of 20%, you probably do not need a graph for this last parameter C. You can say something like: "The results show that the temperature increase with varying parameter C is of 20% and lies between the extreme case of parameter A and B, respectively".

Now I will give you an example of how to explain one set of data fully. The following graph has been produced deliberately with Excel. One of the reasons I took this graph is to describe how this graph can be made more readable.

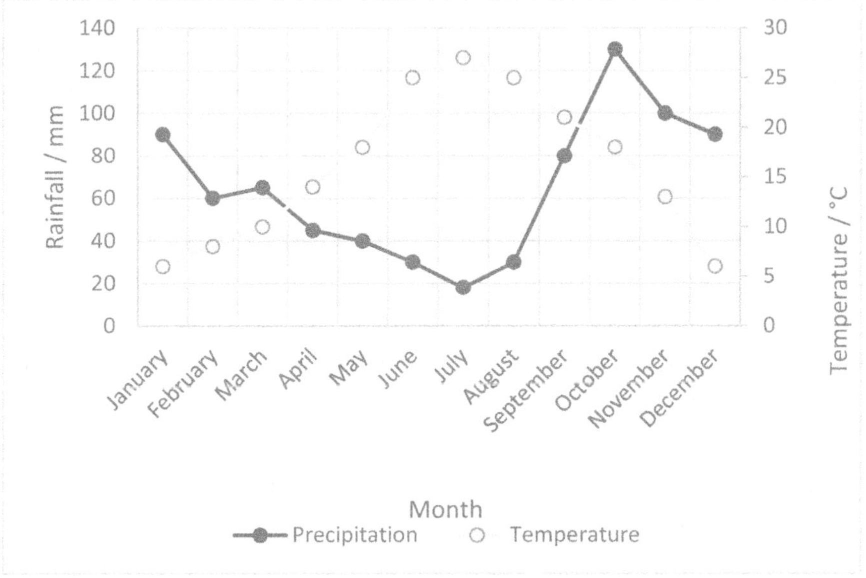

Before we explain and comment on the data shown by the curves in this graph, we will briefly introduce the type of charts and the plotting area. There are two vertical axes. The left axis represents Rainfall in mm and the right one Temperature in °C. The horizontal axis shows all the months in a year. Always put units next to the parameter you plot on an axis. In those cases where you have multiple sets of data to be plotted, it is an excellent idea to use different symbols, lines, line thicknesses, and colors. This will help the reader grasp at a glance that there are various data plotted on the same graph. The previous graph can be improved in the following ways: using two different symbols (circle and square, for instance); use darker colors instead of yellow because, in the print version of the paper, light colors do not appear strong enough. I personally use colors only when I cannot get away with black and white. For instance, here, I would have used two black lines: one continuous and one dashed. As this graph also does, make sure you show in a legend what the two curves represent: one is Rainfall (mm), and the second is Temperature (°C). As this graph did, scale the axis so that all curves use the whole drawing space at their disposal. You do not want to have the same graph plotted with the curves occupying only a portion of the graph's available space. This would not be an efficient use of the paper you print on! Finally, as you can appreciate from the graph above, Excel is not a great plotting tool to present your results. I highly recommend you to get a more professional plotting tool that allows you to customize all things that you plot and see on the graph.

Let's dive in now on explaining the data in the graph. Here is what I would write:

"The temperature of this city ranges between a low of 6 °C in winter months to a maximum of 22 °C in July. There is a slightly more gradual increase in temperature from the winter to the summer months than the more pronounced decrease seen in the fall of last year.

Rainfall reaches the minimum level of around 20 mm when the temperature peaks (July) followed by a steep increase in the next few months approaching nearly 130 mm by October. There is a steady decline in the recorded Rainfall throughout the winter, spring, and early summer. Noteworthy is the bump recorded in March.

The two features of this graph that stand out are the bell-shaped trend of the temperature line and the fact that July is the hottest and driest month of the year."

If you have noticed, I have written enough in the text that you can picture the shape of the curves without watching them. Of course, this is not always possible, and on complex plots, it requires some experience when you describe them in the text. But the general advice remains: the text should describe the plotted data in a way that the reader SHOULD

NOT infer what the data is supposed to show. You must interpret the data you are plotting for the reader to understand it.

CONCLUSIONS

I prefer to write the CONCLUSIONS section before the ABSTRACT. In this section, you make a summary of where you started, what you got, and what that meant, like telling a short story in only a few paragraphs. I have never received any criticism of this part of my manuscripts. Probably because if the reviewers wanted to criticize, they had plenty of opportunities to do so before reaching this section. There are very few journals I came across, which almost dictate the format of this section. They want even references to be dropped in this part of the paper. Additionally, they might ask to clearly show where are the outstanding gaps you can foresee and in which other direction you could take your topic.

ABSTRACT

Why do I suggest you write the ABSTRACT as the last section? Because it is the essence of your work. Like a distillate, here you collect the very cream of all your efforts. You really want to have digested well the presentation of the results and their analysis before you start writing these eye-catching few sentences. At times (especially for Letters), you have a limited number of characters for the ABSTRACT. Sometimes, this can be a daunting task.

The place I start from to write the ABSTRACT is the already written CONCLUSIONS. There I have already condensed the whole paper. All I have to do is to turn a short story into a collection of few but well connected 'sound bites.'

Do NOT underestimate this process, though. The ABSTRACT is your 'business card.' And as such, you want to have it printed not only on good quality paper but plastered it too. It should really shine. Use language to give a nice spin to the work you did so you can portray a captivating image in the mind of the reader and invite the reader to explore the rest of your paper.

Think of what you have done when you have searched for papers to read for your work. You probably went on some search engines and typed some specific keywords. Then a list of possible matches popped up. Now you read the title of those papers and possibly also give a brief look at the authors' names. It is very likely that if the title seems aligned with the work you are doing in your PhD, then you want to read the abstract of that paper. And here it comes. Now you got to the business card the authors of that paper have carefully and diligently crafted. Quite rarely, I have gone over the abstract to find out more if I were not impressed by the abstract, or at least I did not find in the abstract something very well structured and relevant. Experienced authors usually are very skilled at telling good stories, and they can also condense their stories in a few lines only. Even when the work is very technical, these authors have an excellent capability to write for 'effect.'

After talking about Abstracts, I am going to give two examples below from my own published papers and explain what I did with the abstract.

First example:

Standing wave in evaporating meniscus detected by infrared thermography

Cosimo Buffone,[1,a] Khellil Sefiane,[2,3] Christophe Minetti,[1] and Dimitrios Mamalis[2]

[1]*Microgravity Research Centre, Université libre de Bruxelles, Avenue F. Roosevelt 50, 1050 Bruxelles, Belgium*
[2]*Institute for Materials and Processes, School of Engineering, The University of Edinburgh, Edinburgh EH9 3JL, United Kingdom*
[3]*International Institute for Carbon-Neutral Energy Research (I2CNER), Kyushu University, 744 Motooka, Nishi-ku, Fukuoka 819-0395, Japan*

(Received 29 May 2015; accepted 20 July 2015; published online 30 July 2015)

A standing wave has been detected in the evaporating meniscus formed on an organic liquid (acetone) inside a horizontally positioned capillary tube of 1 mm internal diameter. The standing wave is believed to originate from the interaction between surface tension and gravitational forces. We found that the standing wave ensues only at the upper part of the meniscus interface where gravity and surface tension act in the opposite direction. This experimental observation is similar to standing waves observed in floating zones in microgravity but different from travelling waves reported recently in volatile drops; in both cases the waves are produced by temperature differences along a liquid-vapour interface. By employing InfraRed thermography, we recorded the temperature distribution of the meniscus interface, and we found that the first characteristic frequency of the standing wave is around 0.3 Hz. © 2015 AIP Publishing LLC.
[http://dx.doi.org/10.1063/1.4927744]

In the first two lines of this abstract, we clearly said which kind of experiment we made (we even mentioned the tube's size). The second sentence condenses what the physics behind the phenomena might be. Then comes the observation made during the tests. We go on linking our work with the experimental evidence reported by previous researchers. Finally, we mention which tool we used, what we looked at with it, and a peculiar feature we measured (characteristic frequency of the standing wave being 0.3 Hz).

Second example:

Soft Matter

PAPER

Check for updates

Cite this: *Soft Matter*, 2019, 15, 1970

Formation, stability and hydrothermal waves in evaporating liquid lenses†

C. Buffone [*ab]

We present a fascinating experimental investigation of the formation, stability and thermal patterns of evaporating liquid lenses deposited on an evaporating or non-evaporating liquid pool. The use of infra-red allowed measuring the key parameters of the lens and the pool surface temperature. We unveil the significant interaction of the lens with the underlying liquid in the pool. In particular, the contact line of the lens is deformed very significantly and we ascribe this to the combined buoyancy–thermocapillary convection cells on the surface of the liquid pool, generated by a self-induced evaporative cooling effect. We also demonstrate that the evaporative cooling is ultimately responsible for the formation of the lens, which otherwise would have not formed at ambient temperature. The depth of the pool is shown to be very influential on the stability of the volatile lens and its dynamics.

Received 8th October 2018,
Accepted 26th January 2019

DOI: 10.1039/c8sm02044b

rsc.li/soft-matter-journal

In this abstract, note the words I use: 'fascinating', 'significant', 'significantly', 'influential.' These sorts of words wisely inserted in the text convey the importance of the experiment you have performed and especially the findings you are presenting.

Again, in this second abstract, I start with the first sentence telling what my experiment was about. In the second sentence, I say which tool I used to measure what. The next two sentences summarize in a clear way what I observed during the experiments. The following sentence is a crucial point, where I stress the fact that 'evaporative cooling is ultimately responsible for the formation of the lens' and finish this sentence with 'which otherwise would not have formed at ambient temperature'; this is a powerful contrast. The final sentence talks about one key parameter which was varied in the study and, again, descriptively, I anticipate to the reader what s/he would find by reading the full paper.

Note that in this particular example of abstract, no mention of values was made. It is not necessary to insert values of parameters in the abstract.

My last suggestion is that even if you are starting just now to write manuscripts, while you will read lots of papers, you should pay attention to the structure that other authors give their papers and the way they use language to convey their ideas. Let's continue now with the last few left parts of an article.

TITLE

This is an extremely tough part of your story. I typically scan those previously published and very relevant papers to see if I can get some sort of inspiration. You have only a few words to use here for describing your contribution to the field. Ensure that they are very relevant and, crucially, that how you stack them up in this single sentence makes sense in the English language.

Some journals, notably those that publish Letters, put a strict limit on the words or characters count for the title as well. Maybe you want to show your title to a few colleagues to see if they can capture from it what you intend to present in the paper.

REFERENCES

I have been tempted a few times to include a lot of references in my manuscripts. I now think that around 20-25 references are typically more than enough. Your paper is NOT a chronological account of what happened in the history of your field. Your article is also NOT a review paper on the subject, so you do not need to mention a significant number of published works (which can reach a few hundred in review papers). These days you can get from most search engines also the citations that published papers have attracted. Maybe you want also to keep an eye on this for selecting the articles you go citing. But please DO READ the articles you cite. In some cases, the paper cited attracted intense criticism because of the flaws in the authors' work.

I tend to read quite attentively the introduction section of the papers I study. This typically highlights those key papers the authors have cited, and like this, I am automatically directed to other potentially useful articles to read.

When you cite many papers in a row, make sure you mention them in chronological order. I tend to do the same for all the papers I cite in the Introduction, not only those in the same sentence. This gives the reader the impression that you are also aware of how this research field has developed over time.

ACKNOWLEDGMENTS

This is NOT a section where you thank your friends. Lately, journals ask if you have mentioned the funding bodies that gave financial support to your project. You should ask your supervisor for the grant number of the research contract s/he has obtained from these funding bodies.

This seems a trivial thing, but it is not. When you cite the funding bodies from the country you are working in, they get that visibility they deserve on the World stage for the vast sums they invest in both research and you.

Concluding remarks on writing papers

Writing papers is a skill. A skill that you master over time. In case you are a non-native speaker, then this task can be a bit more challenging to start with. However, remember the mantra: 'A voracious reader makes a prolific writer.' Thus, keep reading throughout your PhD project, and writing excellent papers will come naturally to you, even if English is not your first language.

When you read papers, start pulling your head back from the paper/computer screen. What does this mean? Well, deliberately start searching for the overarching structure of the paper you are reading and how the authors use language to tell their stories. This is one particular skill reviewers have developed; they can stand off the manuscript and understand what the authors want to say and how they say it. For reviewers, this is really important because they have to formulate a response, and part of this response is about them telling the authors if there are any flaws in both how the research is done and how the manuscript is written.

I hope that I have covered every part of the paper and that now you feel better equipped at doing the following also with writing papers: 'learning how to learn.'

Publishing your first paper

When I enrolled for my PhD, the kind of rule at my university was that I should produce one journal paper by the end of the program. Universities have specific guidelines for PhD projects, and you should get a copy of these and understand them quite well from very earlier on. Look at how many journal papers you need to publish before you sit your thesis defense and make a suitable plan to achieve that.

In what follows, I will share with you some tips on where to get your work published without being specific about journal names.

With time you will learn how to gauge the quality and impact of your paper. Actually, you will understand pretty well from the time you have spotted something peculiar about your experiment, which quality the resultant article will have. With the first paper, this is less obvious. However, your more experienced supervisor could grasp that in your place.

Each journal has a specific target audience, and it is not unusual that a journal would deliberately target specific geographies and leave others out. For these reasons, you should do some screening of potential journals where your work can find the most suitable home. One way to do this is through your literature search. Unquestionably, you have come across several papers in your specific area. It is somewhat normal to have these papers published in a handful of specialized journals. These journals were the closest fit to the topic the articles tackled. You should carefully think of publishing your papers in those journals as well. Like this, you will have a high chance that people in your field will also read your article. It is customary that experts also favor publishing in a few specific journals, and therefore they also tend to read more those journals they feel connected with. They will keep a close eye on those papers published in these journals and, most likely, will also be regular reviewers of those journals; this means that they might even be reviewers of your paper. Thus, try and spot where these experts close to your topic publish their work. Those journals could be a perfect fit for your manuscript as well. A word of caution is that journals evolve, as we humans also do. And they might change their focus with time. Therefore, search not only old published papers but also newer ones. This will give you a good understanding of the current focus of the journals and how likely these journals would at least consider your work to be published there.

Publishing journal papers has become extremely competitive in recent years. To give you an idea of the eight journal papers I submitted as part of my PhD project, for only one of them, I had to send it to a second journal. And during my project, I tried very hard to spread the papers around to as many good journals as possible. After a long spell in industry, I returned to academia in the middle of 2012. Following an initial steep re-adaptation period in doing research at universities and concentrating on writing papers again, of the work that I produced, only one manuscript had issues being published. I went around three journals before finally publishing it. Since then, things seem to have changed dramatically with publishers. I have seen a significant push from publishers in carefully selecting the manuscript they receive. Some of them want clearly stated justifications why your manuscript should go on 'permanent show' at their venue and the urgency (this latter is a significant matter for Letters). In the last few years, I have also seen journals not liking kind of 'serial' production of papers, meaning papers that are part of an extensive experimental/numerical campaign where you try to publish as you learn about the topic. This is presumably because journals now are literally flooded with manuscripts, and they have problems with space on every single journal issue. Therefore, it is natural that they become much more selective. In theory, by becoming more selective, they should increase the quality of work they publish from researchers worldwide. This is not always true, though.

Journals and publishers have become rather powerful lately. Not only financially but also because of selecting the work that gets published in their journals, they are basically 'dictating' what topics the researchers should focus their attention on. And this might even influence government policy on research grants.

Your institution's geographical location plays a significant role in defying how easy or difficult it will be for you to publish your work. Do some search on the journal webpage, ask your supervisor and other people in your department. They might give you some great tips on this matter.

Today most journals I work with have a rather short review process. I act as a reviewer of several journals (about ten in total) from four large and well-established publishers. When I review a manuscript, the journals give me between ten days (for Letters) and up to thirty days for regular papers. Some other journals, where I occasionally review articles, still have the old three months for the first pass of the review process. There are automatic reminders when there are few days left for me to submit the review. Thus, be reassured that the review of your paper will be rather fast.

Now comes the review process itself. At least two reviewers will be selected to assess your work by the assigned Editor. It is rather common that during the submission process, the online system will ask you for naming between three and five potential reviewers who are familiar with your topic. This is a good chance you have to select someone familiar with your research field who you or your supervisor knows and who will be 'kinder' in reviewing your work. You should be aware that the Editor gets typically paid for his work by the publisher. The publisher receives fees from those readers who read your paper (this also includes your organization who has hosted you to produce the paper in the first place!). You are paid for producing your work. The reviewers are the only people who do NOT get paid for their delicate and crucial task. Reviewers decide if your work gets published or not. And they have a hard time assessing the work of someone else without being able to pose direct questions to the authors. This can be a really tricky task. Other than their professional conduct, at times, reviewers are also confronted with diverse issues as morality and integrity. Overall, reviewers do a rather good job. That said, there are cases (and I encountered less than a handful already) in which the reviewers have not only misinterpreted what I wrote in the manuscript as an author. But at times, it is rather clear that the reviewer had tried his/her best to fail the manuscript. Instead of questioning an assumption I made or a conclusion reached, the reviewer can simply say that he does not believe what you wrote and dismiss your work outright.

Although there are specific reviewer guidelines published by each journal, not all reviewers abide by them. And in those cases where you are failed because of a wrong decision by a reviewer, you typically do not stand a leg in appealing to the Editor. I approached the Editors for three of my manuscripts that I believed were unfairly discarded, and I questioned one of the review reports. In two of those cases, I even appealed to the Editor in Chief for some rather impolite addressing and unfortunate use of words by one reviewer. In the end, nothing happened. It was a complete waste of time for me. And I sincerely discourage you from taking this path. Just search for a different/better venue.

Although this happens sometimes, it is NOT the norm. The majority of reviewers are very polite and courteous. They are very professional, and they would typically write a detailed assessment of your work, as per journal guidelines. In case your manuscript is rejected by one journal, the reviewers' comments are paramount. You should study them and do your very best to address their questions even if you then decide to submit it again to a different journal.

In case the first round of review is positive, then you could also be lucky that no corrections are necessary. In which case, your manuscript is accepted as it is and will go straight into the production process. In my long career as a reviewer, I only received once an exceptionally well-written paper which got published after the first round of review. So, when no corrections are needed, it is more of a unique than a rare case. If, instead, you need to make corrections, there are two scenarios. The first scenario is when there are minor corrections to be done; in this case, it is the norm that the reviewers do not want to check on your minor revisions, and both you and the Editor take responsibility for implementing the corrections. In case you need to perform significant corrections, this is a more involving task. You would need to take each comment from the reviewers and write a response, literally comment by comment. This is usually done on a separate file, and with your response, you will show where in the manuscript you have made changes. Note that you cannot just reply to a reviewer's comment without making changes to the manuscript. You can use either TRACK CHANGES of MSWord or use colored fonts. It must be clear to everyone where in the manuscript you have made changes related to a particular comment by a reviewer. In answer to the reviewers, I typically write the page and starting line in the manuscript where I have made changes. And if you want to really be precise, you can also enter any text you have added to the revised manuscript as an answer to the reviewer's comment.

After you have finished revising the manuscript, you will have several files to send back. They are the original manuscript, the modified manuscript, one file for each reviewer's response, and a letter to the Editor. The journal submission online platform and the Editor message to you will help you figure out what you need to produce and what to upload for the second revision.

It is difficult to know beforehand how many revisions you will go through and if, in the end, your manuscript will be accepted. I had up to three rounds of revisions. And in one case, after the second round of revision, my manuscript was eventually not accepted. From initial submission to manuscript acceptance, there could well be up to six months. This also depends on how quick you are in responding to the reviewers' reports. Thus, factor this in when you plan for your first paper. Maybe you want to make sure you have some other activities starting when you submit your manuscript, so you do not lose any precious time merely waiting.

The final suggestion of this section is PICTH HIGH, but not that high that you break your neck! You should be ambitious and target an excellent journal as a venue for showcasing your work. However, do not try and submit an engineering technical manuscript to the top journals in science. You will waste your time and their time. Take also into consideration that continuous disappointments could turn into sadness, and over time, if you continue pitching wrongly, this might even turn into hopelessness. You MUST do everything possible to avoid feeling powerless. Your mental well-being is KEY for your SUCCESS in the long and at times arduous journey of the PhD project.

After the Checkered Flag — 4

From submitting your thesis until after your thesis defense

Very well done! You reached very far already. Take some time contemplating on this achievement of yours. It is not a small thing; it is a feat. Only after your soul is permeated by the good thoughts you have about what you have done to date, it is probably time to keep reading the rest of this chapter.

We are going to get into a different mindset while you wait for sitting your thesis defense. Are you ready for this other endeavor? If you are ready, then carry on reading. Otherwise, take some extra time to recharge your thirsty racing car.

Getting through the checkered flag does not mean you have reached your final destination in life. Far from it. The PhD is a springboard. It would help if you aimed at using it to climb more and reach further. For this reason, I will give some suggestions on what you can actually do from the moment you submit the thesis to your university up until after your actual graduation.

Let's start with that 'dead' time spanning between the thesis submission and the thesis defense. This part of your project should actually be planned well in advance. The day you submit your thesis, you might feel so much relief that you basically can go into a period of happily protracted inactivity. While you must take some quality days entirely off work, you should not squander this precious time. It feels the same as after having run a long marathon: you need to recover from it physically, mentally, and emotionally as well. Best if you can rest for a couple of days and then go on a short trip somewhere distant where you indeed switch off from all the intense work you have done in all those recent months of typing. Recharging your body with good quality and healthy food, sleep better and longer, and doing some light exercise, will restore your body energies. It is also equally important that you recharge your mind. After all, your brain has been under strain more than your body (which probably has remained mainly immobile during the thesis' writing up phase). How can you recharge your mind? You will be amazed to know that your mind will take much less than your body to recharge. Even under severe distress, your brain is so well equipped that it will basically transfer most of the strain to your body. The most important and more natural way to recharge your mind is to 'slow down.' Literally, slow down. If you slow down your body, your mind will slow down as well, and vice-versa. Therefore, doing soft activities such as yoga, mindful meditation, or simply close your eyes and do nothing at all for say 10-15 minutes at a time. Repeat this 2-3 times a day, and after a few good days, your mind will be completely recharged and ready to go. If you find out that this is indeed a good habit, why not use it in everyday life? I tend to take a couple of walks per day (between 20-30 minutes each), then take many other short breaks during which I stand up from my desk and walk around, even if it is merely walking around the flat or the office. Be mindful that taking a break from typing at your desk and watching YouTube or reading your favorite news online is NOT truly a break. It is merely a temporary switch from doing something in which you are actively performing to another in which you are less actively doing things, but you are still pretty much involved!

Cleaning your flat/office/desk is also a nice break as you use your hands instead of your brain. Your eyes also get a nice break from being bombarded by colors and a flashing screen. If you need to remain seated for a long time in front of the computer, it is advisable that from time to time, you take your sight away from the computer and focus on a distant object for, say, ten seconds. Then you can return your focus on the screen and concentrate on the same remote object after another ten seconds. Repeat these few times, and your eyes will suffer less strain by staring at the screen.

When you know more or less the day you will submit your thesis, you should also plan what you will do after having relaxed for a while. Typically, reviewers will take between one and two months to review your thesis. What can be done in this dead time while you wait? Surely, you can write some papers, or maybe you can start hunting for a new job. Both of these are very time-consuming activities and will more than fill between one and two months you have got at your disposal.

It should be emphasized here that when your supervisor gives the green light to submit your thesis to the university for review, typically, the quality and amount of the work done are deemed more than good enough for you to graduate. Therefore, if you passed this milestone, then there is a high likelihood that you will pass the defense and get those three letters you can use after your name.

A date for the thesis defense will be set, and on that day, you will present your work to the reviewers; the two reviewers (one internal and the other external to your university) will critically assess your work. The reviewers are not going to be very harsh with you. Why? Because usually, your supervisor knows the quality of the thesis you have produced, and s/he has also suggested the names of the reviewers to the university. It goes without saying that you should still be prepared to accept some minor or major criticism. It is rather common that some portions of your thesis must be re-written, some new additions could be necessary, and of course, some parts could even be axed. Take this with some philosophy. Your thesis is like your brainchild, and, understandably, you feel a bit disappointed, especially if you are asked by the reviewers to remove some parts. Be reassured that the reviewers, usually being colleagues of your supervisor, do not have any intention to harm you. They have genuine concerns about your thesis and what they are suggesting you do is NOT a CRITICISM on YOU personally, rather a criticism on how you have conducted your work or how you presented it inside your thesis.

Depending on how many and how vital the reviewers' suggestions are, you will be asked to make the changes and show them only to the internal reviewer. Or, in case there is a lot of work to be done, then both reviewers could demand that you show them the improved version of the thesis. And it works almost exactly as for a manuscript submitted to a journal. With the added benefit of the increased speed and that the reviewers are named, and at least on paper, they are 'more friendly.'

At this point, you go back to your desk (or lab in the unlikely case this is also necessary) and implement all requested changes. You submit the improved version of your thesis, and typically this is the end of your PhD project. Then you will be asked to participate at a later date in the graduation ceremony (which I highly recommend, although I have been the culprit for deciding not to attend it).

This will formally be the end of a very long, at times rather tortuous, undoubtedly highly fascinating, and most likely energy-draining journey. I am pretty sure that for those of you who have been able to navigate through the mist and finished it in relative peace with your supervisor and others around, you would be prepared to do it again. So would I.

Is the PhD an end or a new beginning?

There is no doubt that the PhD is a higher degree that gives a massive boost to your career prospects. In Europe, a PhD is still mainly regarded as a specialization you have obtained. Surely, you will also be treated differently from others who do not have a PhD, but I have seen that people of the same age who seek work in industry in Europe, one with the PhD and the other with a Master, they get pretty much the same salary. However, this is one side of the coin. The other side of the coin is an entirely different story. As time passes, your PhD gains more value even in industry. Top engineering companies, for instance, almost request that their directors have PhDs; a notable country where this happens is Germany. A PhD in Europe might bring you less money than an MBA. Still, an MBA is typically tied to sectors of the economy where there are large capital flows, like in finance and insurance, or more generally in economics.

A PhD in places such as the USA takes you to another planet altogether. In the USA students must foot a significant bill to study in general, and only a small portion of those who get a Master would enroll for a PhD. This is also shown by many immigrants in the USA with doctoral degrees found both in academia and industry. In case you want to really cash in for your efforts, you should consider chasing a job in those countries where gaining a PhD is rather tricky for economic or societal reasons. Other developing countries have specific programs attracting young talents to bring in international experts for training local students and staff; since 1994, one of these countries has been China. Needless to say that it is rather difficult to move within the national borders as typically there are significant cultural, economic, and at times political differences. Let alone moving between neighboring countries or even between continents. The initial 'shock' can be massive, and the adaptation lengthily and painful; this has been my case when moving to

Germany and China. Eventually, after many months I adapted by having understood the local frame of mind, culture, and societal traits. This was rather hard, but I stuck to my mantra that I must hang around with locals to feel fully immersed. In the end, I can confirm that the harder it has been, the more dramatic were the changes I implemented, and ultimately a much better and tolerant person I became.

Now that you have a 'luxury car' in your hands, it is probably a good idea to spend some quality time and research where your PhD can bring you the usual 'bang for your bucks,' we humans should always aim at. Before that, it is probably worth talking about a small detail of some importance. I did not take a few good weeks off after the end of my PhD. I started my first job in industry two days after my thesis defense. I do not regret that, but surely I would have benefitted from some space between these two very different environments. Going from a highly organized university environment located in a charming city where I could tap into training and support resources to a small company of 70-ish people situated in a small town was already a big shock. If we take into account the type of work and how it was done in the two places, it resulted in a challenging first year for me. An additional hurdle was my junior managerial and supervision role of some locally placed PhD students and some young engineers. I must admit it was a hell of a ride!

It is your own choice to decide what is the best career path after your PhD. However, based on my personal experience and that of people I managed or worked alongside, I feel in a position to be able to give some general advice. Here it is. First and foremost, you should understand more about your personality. Your personality traits at this age are well defined already, and they are difficult to change. The way you think, perceive, and behave are characteristic of who you grew up to be. Even if you cannot entirely spot these traits, they are pretty clear to people who have been around you for a while. Thus, if you cannot pinpoint what they are, ask your close friends for a friendly and honest chat about your personality traits. Why is your personality so important? Well, because it pretty much defines the kind of job, you are more likely to excel using the least possible combination of energy and time. Let me give you a couple of examples. The first example is that an anxious person should not be involved in sales. In fact, despite a sales job usually bring more money, it is somewhat stressful. It is full of calls outside regular working hours, with stressed customers who try to pass on you their problems (I know this firsthand because I dealt with many sales managers and customers in my industrial experience). Then you have very demanding targets to reach in a timely way. This is definitely not a job for someone who worries a lot, does not take criticism lightly, and finds it challenging to communicate with others at virtually any time of the day. As a second example, let's look at my personal mistake after my PhD. I wanted to become a company director one day and did not have a clear idea of how I would have achieved that. So, I sought a junior managerial post in my first company. Only to find out that I dealt with people for most of my time and felt between a rock and a hard plate; that was really unpleasant. But this was not all. A few years afterward, I moved to a much bigger engineering company, and, by and large, I found the same issues. Then I started paying attention to the setting, the people involved, and myself. Instead of 'doing,' I started observing more and acting less. I concentrated on my technical work instead of fixing issues that others created and then left behind. To my dismay, I realized that my productivity skyrocketed, and the team, overall, was still performing poorly and probably even slightly better than with my numerous previous interventions. I concluded that my personality traits did not allow me to supervise people at work on an almost daily basis. In fact, after some of them failed to perform (for whatever reason), I would jump on the project and deliver it myself. That is not how a manager in a company setting should do it. The manager does not do it; the manager gets others to do it. After this experience, I had a sales support engineering post in industry before deciding to ditch industry altogether and return to academia. I had a dream to become a company director but not even a sensible sketchy plan for it. And the absence of a clearly defined plan came from the lack of knowledge I had about company managerial routes and my personality traits.

These two examples show you how important it is to choose a career path that suits your personality. You can still excel when choosing a career path that does not match your personality traits. In my case, I was also rather successful (from a technical standpoint) in the jobs I had in industry. But I failed miserably with the desire to become an effective manager.

Now comes the question you might have been waiting for. What is better, an academic or industrial job? This is also a rather personal choice, which should be weighed carefully. As my career to date demonstrates, you can come out of academia and dive into industry and vice versa as many times as you like. At least in principle. However, there are some potential pitfalls that you should be aware of. After spending few years in a specific job function and then jumping across the river (industry to academia or vice versa), you might be asked why you are doing it by the people who hire you. Additionally, you will endure an adaptation period which can last months. The mindsets of industry and academia are very different. The former wants to get things 'out of the door.' The latter tries to get money in the door and then very creatively produces ideas that might only remotely be connected to products and services. Jobs in academia are typically safer than those in industry. In

Industry, you might get more money and possibly also some yearly bonus, a treat you do not usually get in academia. If I had to give you a suggestion, this would be it: do not jump back and forth between academia and industry because the likelihood is that your career progression will suffer a lot. Most of the people who have significant career developments are those who look around for the right place, and then once they have found it, they stick to it for a very long time. Companies and universities are more likely to invest in you after seeing that you are committed to them. Training and development in general cost money and no one is prepared to squander it. The last observation is the rough estimation that shows how a person needs to spend around 10,000 hours to master a new job. If you put a lot of effort into it (meaning working more than 40 hours a week), 10,000 hours would consume more than 4,5 years of your working life! Every time you change your job completely, you need another 4,5 years to become a master in the new position. You can do it over a shorter period, but you will be working outside the recommended number of hours per week. In some countries this is not allowed and working more than 12 hours a day is definitely illegal in most places. Therefore, from a legal standpoint, you cannot work more than 60 hours per week; and even if you worked 60 hours per week, you would achieve the 10,000 hours mark for mastering a new job in almost 3,5 years. Only after this 10,000 hours mark, you can start dreaming of stepping-up a notch in your career in that new workplace.

Further training

During my PhD project, I had a lot of opportunities to be involved in training. I took them all rather as a chance instead of as a burden. Even the laser and chemical hazard training courses were quite informative and well delivered. Today, more than 18 years after those training courses, I am still using that knowledge to warn and guide those people working with me in the lab. I am also better placed to help my people selecting the right training course for them to attend.

Other than health and safety, your university will also have additional training such as Time Management, People Management, and Leadership courses. I would recommend attending Time Management at the very beginning of your PhD as you will use it throughout. For what concerns People Management and Leadership courses, maybe it is better to attend them in the second part of your 3rd year of PhD. These might be more useful after graduation.

There are not only university-based courses but also some off-campus ones. They are not free. But many of them are offered at special rates for PhD students, and research councils sponsor some of these courses. I have been to one of these just after submitting my thesis in the late spring of 2004. It was a SUPERB experience. Something so SPECIAL I still remember it vividly to these days: a jaw DROPPING, eye WATERING, and ears SPLITTING experience of a weeklong breath. It lasted only one full week but felt as never-ending. There were around 100 participants, all final year PhD students, and approximately 15 moderators, among which several lecturers. The program was really full of activities. Primarily indoor but several outdoor activities as well. Most of the events were performed in groups, and the groups were always composed of different people. There were ludic activities such as climbing, singing, blindfolded walking, as well as more serious sessions of CV production, formal interview with proper debriefing and feedback. The interviewers were also students; the moderators helped set the scene and give instructions on how to conduct a mockup interview. I met several young folks from so many different UK cities. I also knew about several students from my university with which I traveled together by train to the meeting place in both directions. And for this feast all that we had to pay was the train tickets, with of course food and beverage for the two legs of the journey from our university to the event location and back.

That was back in 2004. Sixteen years later, the choice you have, of course, is almost unparalleled. Many of these training courses are also online. I suggest you pick some courses which you deem essential for the next 1-2 years of your career. Probably giving priority to those of immediate benefit such as those that would give you increased employability.

Of these, if I were you, I would choose some held in person as well. Human contact will never be entirely substituted by remote interaction. In selecting online courses, I would also pick the ones that offer some interaction between participants. The best would be those online courses where you can interact during the lesson. It might still feel like an old FRONTAL setting in which there is one speaker (the teacher) and many students right in front of him/her. Still, this setting is far better than those in which you can either interact through a written chat or, worse, those pre-recorded lessons in which there is no possibility of interaction at all. This latter should be chosen for specific courses that are almost technical training in which you want to achieve a specific goal. For instance, this is when an almost mnemonic approach is necessary to pass the final test. The chat allows some limited interaction but can be a bit confusing if there are many students/users. By far, the best online course is the first one mentioned in which you can vocally interact with the teacher. My experience of taking such online courses is that there is little interaction between the students, albeit you can interact with the teacher. The teacher is almost always the focal point. If you are paying for the online course, take time to understand how many participants are there. With more than 12-16 participants, you will not benefit a lot from the course: with too many people, the interaction is chaotic.

Whatever your preferences and desires are, keep in mind that training is a kind of lifelong approach. Today most people are required to acquire new skills on an almost constant basis. There are both employer-driven needs and societal ones that will push you to get signed to training courses over the whole duration of your working life and beyond. There are also personal pressures due to life-changing events and experiences that act as a catalyst in literally dragging you from the feet back to a real or virtual classroom for learning more. This lifelong training mentality is now widely accepted as a regular thing all of us should embrace.

Few more suggestions

In this short section, we will briefly mention four small things that can significantly impact your life as a committed and attentive PhD student.

Disaster aversion.

These are some practical suggestions to avoid at least distress if not preventing a disaster from being engulfed by events outside of your control. Let me tell you two stories. During my PhD project, a professor from my same university (I believe to remember he was from Medicine) was traveling from home to work by bus. Well, after he stepped out of the double-decker bus, he realized he left the laptop on the bus. Soon after came the awful news that it was not possible to recover the missing laptop. I read from the news that a sizable cash prize was set up for who handed in the laptop, because it contained almost ten years of data and files from this professor's work. A lab caught fire in a separate case in a different university, and all items inside the lab were destroyed. With the hardware, also soft copies of tests performed and written reports went up with the smoke.

As these examples demonstrate, there is nothing we can actually do to eradicate such disasters. But we can put in place preventive measures to avoid that all our work gets lost. One way to do this is to make regular back-ups of your files and keep several copies in very separate places. For instance, you can keep one copy in your office, one copy inside your lab, and one copy at home. Nowadays, you should also consider uploading files on the cloud. Right after I heard about the two stories I mentioned above, I made back-ups every 3-4 months using RW-CD-ROMs, which were the preferred recording media at the time. These days with affordable large external drives, you can do this every month. I have kept that learned habit on and do regular back-ups to these days.

Good practice.

You will probably build several set-ups of your experiment. You might want to consider documenting the tests you do (also taking pictures or videos) and make some drawings/sketches of the layouts. If you do this, why not also document the test procedures? All of this upfront effort will come in very handy during the writing time for both papers and thesis.

Keep a detailed list of items you bought and where you got them from with the salesperson's contact details. This can be very useful also for your future career. I still use these details of suppliers I have first bought items from 15-20 years ago. It is like keeping their business cards in a folder. And you will be surprised as most of these folks remember you as good as you remember them.

Most likely not needed.

Do you actually need to print all the papers you read? I loved holding the paper in my hands, also because my eyes did not get stressed much by looking at a screen for long time. Now I do not do it anymore. Screens are no longer made of cathodic tubes, and my eyes get much less tired. Then there is the moral question of the impact of our actions on the environment. Paper is costly to produce and especially to recycle, but the inks used to print on it are polluting. Removing the inks (which have metal components in them) from paper, uses acids which are pollutants themselves. I am even trying hard to switch from pens to pencils when I write. Pens' juice is also ink, and as such, it pollutes as well.

The well-lit layout.

What we see has a massive influence on how we perceive things. Have you ever considered how important is what our eyes see? We try to watch with our eyes, but even all of that background around the focus of our attention is tremendously important for our well-being. Try to live and work in rooms which have enough light in all directions, ceiling included. Then, say, once every six months, why not changing your sitting position by changing your desk's location or the layout of the whole room. If you are offered to change the office or the lab during the PhD project, I suggest you take such an offer. Remaining in the same place for long contributes to mental laziness and unwillingness to embrace changes.

Want to become a writer?

Your thesis might be your First Fully Fledged book you wrote. It might not be the last. It should not be the last time you transferred your best thoughts and ideas on paper/screen.

Writing can be a gratifying thing. I take writing as a way to put order into my thoughts. When I write, it is like I am talking aloud. And I can see my thoughts pictured as well as hearing the sound they make because, most of the time, when I write, I also whisper out. I also consider writing as talking to a great friend. A friend that is not judgmental. A patient friend. A friend who does not mind me scribbling, crossing, and erasing as many times as I like.

Depending on what you are writing and why you have decided to write, writing can also be a more orderly way to vent from disappointments, deal with frustration, and even manage anger. History is filled with great minds that endured impossible drama and were able to turn their never-ending personal tragedy into a spectacular never-ending production of incredibly beautifully crafted masterpieces for the never-ending delight of the entire humanity. One of these cases is master German composer Ludwig van Beethoven. It is believed that he suffered from a rhythmic heart disorder. And, if this was not a bad thing already, some think he also had schizophrenia, which is one of the most debilitating mental disorders. He was allegedly very awkward with others. Even his most famous portrait shows how austere his look was, and in portraits like this one of Beethoven, we now know people could 'fake' how things really were. Despite the seriousness of his condition, he wrote nine incredible symphonies, some of which have become the cornerstone of classical music. Then he wrote hundreds of other compositions. Just pay attention to the number of symphonies he wrote: nine! You need a few very talented composers to write as much as he did, without taking the composition's quality as a comparison tool. There are parts of his compositions in which he shows with music how his sick heart functions (https://theconversation.com/did-beethoven-have-an-irregular-heartbeat-diagnosing-the-composer-through-his-music-36113). In one of these beautiful pieces of music, he takes humankind through the slowing down of his failing heart to a sudden stop. A long pause ensues, followed by what listeners experience as an almost resuscitation. What comes after is nothing less than a feast of sounds for our ears. How on Earth this man was able to turn his human tragedy into such incredibly beautiful pieces will probably remain an equally significant legacy he left besides classical music itself. When his earing started failing him, he did not stop at all. He started placing an ear to the floor and feeling his piano's vibrations transmitted through the piano's legs into the floor and eventually reaching his brain. This incredible man defies the myth that severe psycho-physical impediments have to be barriers for humans. He demolished all possible obstacles that Nature put on his path.

In order to write, you need to give some order and sense to the continuous bombardment by which your brain is sieged because of the bursting of thought bubbles that pop up randomly. If you place some attention, you might conclude that you cannot stop all these thoughts coming up in your brain. You are absolutely right! Nobody can stop these thoughts from popping up in our brains. This is why if bad thoughts dominate the stage in your brain, it becomes quite challenging to control them. Now let see how you can channel those thoughts in a direction and in a way that you exploit them instead of being exploited by them. The first thing you need to consider is that you have to learn how to develop those thoughts. They are raw thoughts. Sometimes with little or no effort, these thoughts might become great concepts/ideas. But even at this stage, they might not be developed enough for you, or for anybody else to be of any substantial and tangible use. Then, the question remains: how do we leap to the next stage? The answer to this fundamental question is READING. Ok, we have understood that reading is the key, but you might still ask why? Let's have a closer look at it.

By reading other people's work, you literally pick up the best their brain produces. The associated step with reading a lot is that you start making connections between all you learn. And this is the stepping stone that leads to enhanced intelligence. Intelligence is defined as the capability of all humans to apply to a new field that they have learned into a different area. The more you know, the more connections your brain makes between these different ideas and facts you learned about.

There is another part of your brain that will unleash your creativity. This is the emotional part of the brain, which is located in the right part of the brain. When you unleash this part of you, you will become more emotionally intelligent. And this will literally propel you to new heights. To achieve this, you need to work on letting your emotions out. If you can also achieve getting them out in a non-destructive way, this would grant you almost full control of how you feel, think, and behave. This one is not a simple task. It requires a lot of practice and some reading about how the brain works, which I highly recommend you for improving your life quality in general.

All of this put together allows you to capitalize on your thoughts by developing them, transferring them on paper, and eventually exploiting them. When this full cycle is completed, then you are in a position to decide if writing is for you. That is the journey I made. I did not know this would have been where I would have ended up, but looking back, I can spot now all the steps I took to get where I am. And I feel rather good to be at the place I have reached.

It is like when you start learning a new language. One of your biggest blockers is your limited vocabulary. You need to read a lot to assimilate the meaning of new words as they are put into context inside phrases. Then, you start assembling sentences which might well have misplaced words. It takes another great leap to begin mastering the sentences' structures and even how to connect the paragraphs using the linking words. While you learn this, you also start picking up how to use language for effect. As in the case of expressing emotions, you will 'laugh' when your eyes start 'seeing' the humor and sarcasm embedded in sentences of the new language you are learning. By now, even those apparently inert, at times weird, and randomly bundling of words inside the idiomatic sentences make you fully grasp what they mean. Over time, if you are fully immersed in the new language, you naturally will start thinking in the new language. Eventually, even your emotive expressions would come out in the new language enriched by the knowledge of both languages you have mastered, and you can now speak fluently.

Continuing reading is key to produce lots of words needed to become a prolific writer. You would also need to understand the structure of the kind of writing you will be involved in. A novel is different from poetry, and fiction is very different from scientific writing. They all have a structure, and you need to understand what that is to become a competent writer.

There is yet another aspect that thrills me when I decide to write something. It is the feeling that I am passing my knowledge and experience to people living now and future generations. This is one reason why writing on stones inside caves was developed: the most knowledgeable people in the tribe wanted to make illustrated pictures of hunting settings so new generations could be trained by watching the drawings and being assisted by their tutors. The one of hunting was a skill that defined the survival of the tribe. I take that challenge on, and when I write, I tend to pour on paper/screen literally everything I can squeeze off my brain.

I wish to say here that other than just writing, you should find a strong motive to do that. Ask yourself for what reason do you want to write? Who do you want to reach with your writing? How do you want to reach your readers? Why should they be interested in picking up your brain from your writings?

Once you have found the target audience, start mastering the structure of the type of writing that this audience is craving to read.

From all the writers and readers of this world, I want to thank you for all your endeavors.

Good luck!

Bibliography

Caro S., How to Publish Your PhD, SAGE Publications Ltd., 2009.

Glasman-Deal H., Science Research Writing for Non-Native Speakers of English, Imperial College Press, 2009.

Kimsey-House H., Kimsey-House K., Sandahl P., Whitworth L., Co-Active Coaching, Nicholas Brealey Publishing, 2018.

Kline, S. J. and McClintock, F. A. (1953). Describing the uncertainties in single sample experiments. Mechanical Engineering, pages 3–8.

Moffat, R. J. (1988). Describing the uncertainties in experimental results. Experimental Thermal and Fluid Science, 1:3–17.

Silvia P. J., Write It Up: Practical Strategies for Writing and Publishing Journal Articles, Amer. Psychological Assn., 2014.

Whitmore J., Coaching for Performance, Nicholas Brealey Publishing, 2017.

Williams P. and Menendez D. S., Becoming a Professional Life Coach, W.W. Norton & Company, 2015.

https://www.timeshighereducation.com/news/phd-completion-rates-2013/2006040.article, last accessed 13 August 2020.

https://en.wikipedia.org/wiki/Big_Five_personality_traits, last accessed 13 August 2020.

https://pdfs.semanticscholar.org/679f/6146dce2b5fb9927c21acdae176570157360.pdf, last accessed 13 August 2020.

https://www.teachermagazine.com.au/articles/problem-based-learning-and-project-based-learning, last accessed 13 August 2020.

https://www.merriam-webster.com/dictionary/research, last accessed 13 August 2020.

https://en.wikipedia.org/wiki/History_of_scientific_method, last accessed 13 August 2020.

http://marcprensky.com/wp-content/uploads/2013/04/Prensky-Achievement-vs-Accomplishment-FINAL.pdf, last accessed 13 August 2020.

https://theconversation.com/did-beethoven-have-an-irregular-heartbeat-diagnosing-the-composer-through-his-music-36113, last accessed 13 August 2020.

www.ingramcontent.com/pod-product-compliance
Lightning Source LLC
Chambersburg PA
CBHW051517030726
47592CB00006B/2309